PALPABLE CLOCK

Mulberry Poets & Writers Association
P.O. Box 468
Scranton, PA 18501

PALPABLE CLOCK
25 Years of Mulberry Poets

Gerard Grealish
Karen Blomain
Nancy K. Deisroth
David Elliott

Editors

Scranton: University of Scranton Press

Library of Congress Cataloging-in-Publication Data

Palpable clock : 25 years of Mulberry poets / Gerard Grealish ... [et. al.], editors.
    p. cm.
 ISBN 1-58966-106-0 (pbk.)
 1. American poetry--Pennsylvania--Scranton Region. 2. American poetry--Pennsylvania--Wilkes-Barre Region. 3. Pennsylvania--Poetry. I. Grealish, Gerard, 1947- II. Mulberry Poets & Writers Association.
 PS549.S3P35 2004
 811'.54080974837--dc22

                                  2004061204

Distribution:

**University of Scranton Press
Chicago Distribution Center
11030 S. Langley
Chicago IL 60628**

Contents

Preface

I was living in Manhattan—on Sullivan between Bleecker and West 3rd in the West Village—when I attended my first poetry readings in 1968, 1969. At St. Mark's, I heard Robert Lowell and Allen Ginsberg give a joint reading—learned, a week later, that the drunk in the audience heckling Lowell for being an "academic" was the irascible beat poet Gregory Corso. For the most part, I attended open readings held in storefront spaces, community halls, church halls, etc. I don't remember exactly where they were now and doubt they still exist. I remember rooms and folding chairs, the heat and sweat of summer. There, in those poorly ventilated venues, the whirring fans were shut off once someone stood before his or her audience to read or recite from memory. It was important that the poetry be heard, no matter how good or bad it was.

The open readings provided a chance to see and hear people who had something to say—often the exotic kind of people I'd be attracted to on the streets and wonder about, or sometimes people who looked pretty conventional but weren't once you heard them speak. They offered a chance for me to get up before a group and nervously read some of the stuff I had recently put on paper. The audiences were kind for the most part, applause usually easy to come by. In later years, I'd learn that the poet Paul Blackburn, who wrote with passion and translated poetry from the Provençal, frequented these readings himself. I think I remember a guy everyone seemed to know. When I see photos of the late Blackburn, I swear that was the guy.

I was 21, just out of the University of Scranton, where I had written a couple of poems that got published in the college literary magazine, *Esprit*, protested against the Vietnam War, and enjoyed feeling myself a member of the more artistic and offbeat fringe of the student population. I was "digging" this poetry scene in the West Village, the East Village, definitely digging the jazz scene, where, for a $2.50 minimum, you could sit at the Top of the Gate (the Village Gate, that is) and hear the likes of

Ahmad Jamal, Charlie Mingus, and Cedar Walton. By 1970, when I had left the city and returned to northeastern Pennsylvania, the seeds of what has become the Mulberry Poets & Writers Association (MPWA) had been sown.

In 1977, Karen Blomain asked me, along with David Elliott, to join her in a project she was piloting: a poetry reading series that would bring to Scranton, on a regular basis, America's most accomplished and well-known poets. Having organized a successful reading by poet Milton Kessler at the Jewish Community Center in Scranton, Karen had approached her good friend Dorothy Reddington, then president of the Friends of the Scranton Public Library, about the library support group sponsoring a continuing series of such readings. Thanks to Dorothy and Karen, the Scranton Public Library Poetry Series was inaugurated, and thanks largely to Carol Gargan, David Elliott, and Karen, the series continued. Poets such as Louise Gluck, W. S. Merwin, Mary Oliver, Tess Gallagher, Marie Howe, Michael S. Harper, Galway Kinnell, Lynn Emanuel, Robert Creeley, Jane Augustine, Gary Snyder, Lawrence Ferlinghetti, Toi Derricotte, Etheridge Knight, Eamon Grennan, and Cornelius Eady would give readings in the Lackawanna Valley. In the Scranton Public Library can be found a priceless archive of videotapes that memorialize the great and historic readings given by these and other award-winning poets in Scranton.

It was an exciting time. Carol Gargan, my wife at the time, joined me during forays into Manhattan on occasion. We'd go to poetry readings at Chumley's, a poetry bar in the city. I was struck by the dimly lit ambiance, where you could sit with an iced mug of beer in front of you and listen, in a laid-back way, to a poet inflecting his or her lines. With the upcoming inception of the major-poet reading series on my mind, it occurred to me that there should be a counterpart, a forum where local poets and writers could showcase their works before a local audience, just like those open readings I'd go to in the Village. Whereas The Friends' presentation of major poets might require a more formal venue to legitimize poets as "celebrities" for the general public, it seemed to me that the perfect setting for a series where locals could read to their friends and other local writers and get to know one another in an informal manner would be a pub.

Enter Paul Scanlan. Scanlan's Saloon on Mulberry Street in Scranton was a hangout not only for local collegians from the University of Scranton and Marywood University but also their aging alumni and other residents from the local community. Paul, apart from providing a congenial Irish atmosphere in his saloon, made clearly the best chili in town. While his establishment tended to get packed and loud, sometimes rowdy, with the jukebox blasting in the evenings, Saturday afternoons were reasonably light, with only an occasional roar from the bar when the Fighting Irish, broadcasted on the bar TV, scored a TD in a close game. Next to "the barroom" was a room with a modest seating capacity of about 50 people, set apart from the bar itself by a half-wall dividing the two rooms. What could be more perfect, I couldn't help thinking.

So I, being a regular enough frequenter of the saloon and a devotee of Paul's chili, sez to him one day, "Paul, would ya be kind enough to entertain the prospect of having poetry readings in yer fine establishment one Saturday afternoon per month in that quaint room to the left of yer bar? I just might be able to bring ya in 30 additional customers on that occasion to suck down yer suds and spoon down yer perfectly spiced chili." To which Paul sez, "Why sure, Jerry, why not, we'd be glad to have ya!"

Ah. It was a match made in purgatory with certain heavenly moments! In the month of September 1978, the *Scranton Sunday Times* carried a full-page "Focus" article announcing in bold headlines that "Bards in the Bar" was due to begin the following month at Scanlan's Saloon on Mulberry Street. Carol created a striking poster, featuring a crescent moon with a woman's captivating face emanating from the lunar curve. "Poets & Writers at Scanlan's Saloon," it announced on the top portion with the crescent, and, on the bottom segment, it provided the schedule of readers for the fall season. The poster adorned key store windows and bulletin boards throughout the town (as would, for many years, a series of memorable Carol Gargan portrait posters of the major poets who read for the Scranton Public Library Poetry Series). And, in October of 1978, it began.

I remember now that first event vividly. I carried with me, as I did for the remainder of that first season, a box full of vigil candles to add a bit of "Bohemia" to the tables of what was to become our poetry reading room, and the matches to light them. I carried a wooden stool for the reader to sit on, which would be placed under the sound speaker in the far back corner of the room, and a clip-on light that could be affixed on the speaker above the seated reader's head so he or she could read poems from the printed page. I brought a ten-gallon hat for donations to cover the overhead and buy drinks for the featured readers. And that was it. No applications for grants. No rental space fees. No readers' fees, other than what was in the hat and might buy a few beers.

I was surprised to find William Bronk, subsequent winner of the American Book Award in 1982, seated at the bar near the entrance when I walked in that first day. I had arranged for him to read in the library series of major poets and had met him on a couple of occasions by then. He knew I was reading at the first event and came down from Hudson Falls, New York. In the course of that first season, both Michael Heller and Gilbert Sorrentino, poets I had studied with, were good enough to read for the series. Both attracted larger crowds than usual and served to keep the momentum of the series going. My good friend Brian Quinn assisted me a great deal in that first year, helping me decide who should read (even helping me carry the aforementioned props into the saloon on the appointed days). He read himself, and a very fine reading it was.

Did I imagine this thing to last as it has? No, to be honest, though I never went so far in my thinking as to envision its end either. When I hitchhiked from Scranton to Alaska in the summer of 1979, I left the previously planned Bastille Day celebration of Poetry and Jazz in the hands of my friends Rondo Semian and Bernie McGurl. Thanks to them, poetry and jazz rang out from a place called Rabbity Hill Farm that summer, a Woodstock of a different type on the outskirts of Scranton, a beautiful pastoral setting as I remember it. Even as I gutted fish on the Kenai Peninsula, I wished I could have been there hearing it all, seeing the hills roll green beyond the barn. Thanks, guys.

Past presidents and officers? Others who were helpful? There were many. In its second year, Rondo and Bernie moved the series from Scanlan's Saloon to the Wine Cellar, another bar on Mulberry Street, and changed Poets & Writers at Scanlan's Saloon to Mulberry Poets & Writers Association, a name that has stuck to this day. Timmy and Terry O'Toole, the owners of the Wine Cellar, accommodated us for several years. Their bar was a great meeting place for friends and music. Ray Emanuel, Tara Finnerty, Kate Conahan, and others managed the organization in those early years. Later, Charlotte Ravaioli was at the helm for six years, Jack McGuigan for four, Ann Chmil for two, and recently, Rondo Semian for three. Every time it looked like MPWA was on the brink of extinction, someone stepped up. It's absolutely amazing. It has its own life force, it seems.

Thus, it is only fitting that we celebrate MPWA's silver anniversary with this anthology. As I write this, we are already nearing the completion of its 26th season, but 25 years of existence should not pass without some tangible memento for reaching such a milestone. This book embodies the work of many of the poets who have been featured at MPWA events over the last quarter century—from the very first season through the 25th—a kind of time capsule, a palpable clock of our existence. To those who have left our fold and could not be located for inclusion, it is our sincere wish that they are spreading MPWA seeds in distant, even obscure realms. We have taken the liberty of including a few poets from events of the 26th season to suggest a glimpse of the future, a continuity that MPWA just might ride to a golden anniversary in its 2027-28 season.

The editorial board has attempted to represent in this collection some of the best work that has emerged from the poets who have passed through our ranks over the years. In doing so, we were interested not necessarily in the poems that were read at the particular events poets were featured in (indeed, for many poets included here, the quality of their work has evolved way beyond the poems of the early years) but poems the poets themselves considered representative of their body of work or current work. Any editorial board has a bias that is a product of its own composition, and ours was no different, though we attempted, as best we could, to be eclectic yet consistent in the quality of the work we selected. In the end, we feel quite good about the overall worth of what we have compiled here.

A regional organization such as ours has to be sensitive to its membership. In our attempts, from the beginning, to provide a forum for local writers and, at the same time, a vehicle for development of writers, we have, during the course of our events, allowed for work of varying quality. We have walked this tightrope to encourage free expression, on the one hand, and, on the other, to promote skillful use of language and effective forms of communication. We often offered writing workshops for this reason, sometimes conducted by major poets borrowed from the library series (some of whom are represented in this anthology). From such a mixed pool, latent talent is often discovered and nurtured. In the end, we must thank all those who tried as well as all those who succeeded. Indeed, we must thank all those who never read at our events but nonetheless sat in our audiences and appreciated what we were doing. All were part of the fabric of MPWA and account for its continued life.

The life I speak of is not an abstract hollow of time floating in empty space. Rather, it is a collective force of fleshed-out thought and emotion, of events and relationships, of place, translated and incorporated into language, turning on a phrase, even a word. Those of us who have come together to form the MPWA community share insights borne by perfect words resonating in our brains, the phonetics of language coursing in our blood. Poetry, written and spoken, is alive for us.

Finally, allow me to acknowledge I am honored that the other editors of this volume chose a phrase from one of my poems as the title. Of course, it is less about me than all of us together. *Palpable Clock* demonstrates through its poems that time can have substance inextricably interwoven with its minutes. Indeed, we would hardly know of time apart from the tangible world we encounter; we would not know it to be other than ourselves.

Gerard Grealish
June 11, 2004

Acknowledgments

No work of this kind is birthed unassisted, and the editors wish to express appreciation to the many people who have helped make it possible.

This anthology project is supported by a generous donation from Dennis Toomey and a subsequent matching grant from Altria Group, Inc., through its employee involvement program. In addition, this project and our 25th anniversary season were assisted by generous individual donations from Carrie and Jim Gordon.

Over the past quarter century, MPWA events and projects have been supported by grants from the Pennsylvania Council on the Arts, the Scranton Area Foundation, the Pennsylvania Humanities Council, and the Lackawanna County Arts to the People Program. Since 2001 MPWA has been involved in a community partnership with Keystone College. MPWA also acknowledges their longstanding association with WVIA-FM and its commitment to promoting the literary arts.

Special thanks are extended to Rondo Semian, MPWA President, for his untiring efforts on behalf of the group, and especially for his grant-writing skills; Barb Semian, MPWA's graphic artist, for her many hours of work and her expertise in the full prepress preparation of the manuscript; to Jennifer Hill-Kaucher, Wordpainting, for her creative page layout and cover design; and to Stephanie Stamm, intern, for her capable handling of the correspondence of the editorial board, as well as her fine editing and organizational skills.

Finally, the editors wish to thank the University of Scranton Press for its assistance in bringing this volume to life, and, particularly, to Richard W. Rousseau, S.J. and Patricia A. Mecadon for their continued interest and guidance.

* * *

 This project is supported by Pennsylvania Partners in the Arts (PPA), the regional arts funding partnership of the Pennsylvania Council on the Arts, a state agency. State government funding comes through an annual appropriation by Pennsylvania's General Assembly and from the National Endowment for the Arts, a federal agency. PPA is administered in this region by the Scranton Area Foundation.

Scranton Area Foundation
Catalyst for Community

PALPABLE CLOCK

The Suit of Women
for Erin

This will be our place, this field
we are crossing, a place for the dumb bodies of women.
It will be made for us like a bed. Lost gloves look like hands
in the sprawl of the refuse. Can we forgive
ourselves for running out of light? We follow the skein of
        the river
through the dark, toward pinpricks of porch lights.

We feel the mistake of our skirts, bare legs, in the grope
        of headlights.
The pick-up truck, its empty bed like a furrowed field,
two men in the front seat, driving the river,
wheels straddling the cinder path. Our scattered clothes
        would look like women.
Who would be able to forgive
our leaving the house, turning the doorknob with our hands?

Like paper dolls we are fused, hand to hand.
There is no other trick with scissors that delights
like cutting through folds of paper. Your mother forgave
the litter of odd-shaped confetti, the low table a field
safe for little girls. We are so clearly cut as women—
the long hair, ribbons shimmering like the river.

The land is heavy with water, drinking from the river,
a sodden quilt, with patches of broken glass. For our hands
there would be only the armor of thimbles—the suit of women,
protecting one finger tip in the dimming parlor light.
The cloth smells of skin, a sweat-scented field,
the embroidery hoop skews the grain, fabric gives.

Do we understand this grip? Forgive
our bodies greasy with sweat, slick as the river?
It is that feeling in dark parking lots that were once fields.

I place my keys between my fingers, try to make hands
that could defend me, walking from streetlight to streetlight.
Two of us, women

walking at night, careless women
not counting our hours. Will these men forgive
us? We look to the farmhouses, boxes of light—
we would stay inside forever, but the river
divides them from us, and the truck is not stopping,
        door handles
lying flat, wheels carrying mud to another field.

Stitch these scraps: two women in a field,
with no relief, no giving way of the locked hands,
fear caught in gold-threaded light, in the satin of the river.

On Renoir's *Sleeping Girl with a Cat*

I want to know
she is not dead.
Soon she will wake, and hungry,
reach for bread, pears,
whatever is on the table.
Or maybe she is not sleeping
but waiting, and her eyes ache—
behind her lids is the color
of the painter's backdrop—
light faltering through blood and skin.
She cannot see herself in this painting.
At least after death
the cool metal of coins would salve her eyes.
She wants to be sleeping,
and I want her dream to be about
the flowers in her hat, each petal
elongating into barbs, stems hard
as cartilage, sharpening to quills.
The painter pulled one soft sleeve
off her shoulder, gently as if
he might smudge her skin.
The skirt is loose between her legs,
the way sheets cover furniture,
and there is the cat gray in her lap.
She is sitting still, as much
for the cat as for the man.
The fur smells of dirt and leaves,
and later the girl will find
hairs on her skirt, threads too short
for a needle, nothing that can be
stitched into place, nothing useful.

It Is Better in the Train Station

When lovers are splitting apart
it is better if the last good-bye
is said in the train station

In the train station despair is poured
and transfigured
within oversized spaces
dignified with Corinthian capitals
melted with choreographies
of conspicuous crowds
and hidden sorrows

In the train station
anguish can be rooted in a memory
with the lazy detachment
of the train car

Airports and cafés
leave the last good-bye helpless
the resulting grief unsheltered

It is better if the last good-bye
is said in the train station

Using the Tools of My Ancestors

I strike a chisel against masonry
precisely, surer than I can believe.
The fifty-year-old mortar Dad laid does
not yield easily. But I strike—chink chink,
and wonder where I acquired this manual skill.
It was not in my lifetime, me,
skinny, sedentary, scholarly;
not mason, bricklayer, setter of tile,
like my ancestors for generations.

The modern physicist, Richard Feynman,
said a particle goes from A to B
over every possible path, it sums
over all histories. Was it me striking
the chisel against mortar when Father,
Grandfather or Great-grandfather was against
another stone wall? Or their ancestors
down in the dark, damn mines against coal?

I have been in the attic in total darkness.
Struck nails squarely, pounded them straight in.

Two College Students

I've seen genius so fixed on itself
as to be monkeys, squealing
wicked-itchy
watching a record whirl
in the same drugged circle
33 and 1/3—circa 1969

This—their eternal brilliant conclusion
their $e = mc^2$
this—their Final Solution
their inner-spring of convoluted complexity
as the hands of their clocks
fly off, striking me in the face

Alas!
—the equation that would solve
the mystery of whistling "Dixie"
that would feed the dogs
and "seize the day"!

This penetrated groove
This—track
eternally diminishing
toward a point on a label
at which two loins intersect

and then . . .
. . . cease to be. . . .

Recorded History

Above us
the creaking
breaker
long-legged bird
that doesn't fly
nested in the life
of this town.

Railroad tracks
tied and un-
tied
twisted whips
running beside
the river
in the sun.

I follow the sound
of whistle.
I pucker my lips
WHOOO.

The train huffs the incline.

Clacking air
traps us beside it. Cinders
tick
our cheeks.

She grabs my arm
the *ooooooooooh*
of her mouth
changing to a *nooooo*
word

never
never
never
gooooo here

pulls my shoulder—
hear me
humps of pea
chestnut
spilling behind the cars

the glitter of dark
shards rattles
down the track
and I do.

After supper
women pick loose
coal from slag
along the track

carry it home
in their aprons
like wild onions
chicory
chamomile
like dandelion greens.

Hunting pinkies
they smell the earth
study the fluted
underside
the color of caps
mouths in hard
oooohs
of concentration

warning
each in season
the mistake

of wrong time
and what cannot be used
what spoils
what poisons.

Grandmother
in the garden
pruning roses.
New sister in the basket.
We all startle
at the noon blast.

Later under the lilacs
she tells me
of the day
the sky went black
with the ceaseless shriek,
her father killed
in the cave-in.

The men hauled up
the *ooooohs*
of their blanched lips
struggling
to gill air
out of darkness.

OOOOh
she moans at night
in her room,
the very old one
whose fingers rest
as if they are holding
something round
cannot open
even for the beads.

The little ones
fear her toothless hole
the way the skin sways
under her arms
like unpuffed balloons
swooning for air.

It is 1950
and my eyes
have just
unstuck

and what place
this is
what this darkness
shrill and keen
will mean
comes slowly.

I eat it
like the plate
of boiled greens
because it is placed there
in front of me
and because I have
no will
until later
when I have the words:
Lackawanna
for river
Archbald
for this place by three bridges
Number 5—the mine
until the old woman
lies in the box
in the living room.

I wake upstairs
in the night.
The candle left burning
in the hallways
before the picture
of the Sacred Heart
since the day
of long-screeching
spikes crow shadows
above my path
to the kitchen.

And my throat
opens
to its first crooning
woman story:
the plain song
of this place
what the women made
what they gathered
what they told

I eat it
I chew it
I turn it into myself.

The Wrecking Ball Visits Lackawanna Avenue

A thousand centuries
Of the bones of trees
To blend smoky heat
Of coal and whiskey
Into this black street

These bricks
Pressed from the foreheads
Of hungry immigrants
Into churches and banks
A hundred thankless years ago

The steel ball like a dark sun
Swings from a menial boom
Into these ostensibly obsolete walls
To make room for the graves
Of another negligible past

Asterisk
(*Apologia ad Infinitum*)

A time when I'm walking
The dog at night
Under a clear sky full
Of lights and hope
Reminding me of
Restlessness and ease

There is now the fact
That my glass was
Half full, then half empty,
Then half full again,
And again, until I was
Drunk again in a page
Less reasonable and feared
Than this one

Where inside it is
Warm because that is
Where loved ones sleep
And outside it is cold
Because it is winter
And I deserve to see
The error of my ways
In the shapes of my breath

And surely it is an
Asterisk from God, blinking
Up there, patiently waiting
For me to find the footnote
That goes with it to explain,
Somewhere in the endless
Bibliography of stars

An Old Woman's Ears in Temple

Fragile and beautiful
A maze of folds
Flowers of skin
The old woman's ears
Point to a hope

Behind her as she leans
Forward to amplified prayer
In a sabbath hour
Amid so many empty seats
In the sanctuary

I stare away from the words
On the page in the book
To the silent hymns
Of delicate flesh singing
Notes scored on wisps
Of thin hair

A fugue of grace
Soundless in the loud
Synagogue air
Dancing in wild stillness
To the music of commandments
We can't read or hear

Día de Todos los Santos

El sol se ocultó ese día
sin que nadie lo notara.
La luna se hizo pedazos
y el mundo siguió su marcha.
Sólo Yerma y Marianita
y unos poetas lloraron
porque ese día Granada
se bañó en sangre Lorquiana.

All Saints Day

The sun disappeared that day
and no one noticed.
The moon shattered itself;
the world ignored it.
Only Yerma and Marianita
and some poets cried in anguish
for on that day, Granada
bathed itself in Lorca's blood.

Dissolution

Cutting a rectangle with the spade
we slowly lift a scalp of grass.
Deepening the hole we made
through layers of life and dust we pass.

We slowly lift a scalp of grass,
our minds considering the fall;
through layers of life and dust we pass
to the extinction of us all.

Our minds, considering the fall,
attempt to fathom shoebox graves;
to the extinction of us all
we dwell on lives we couldn't save.

Attempt to fathom shoebox graves
in twilight, down on muddy knees;
we dwell on lives we couldn't save
and fear we came here to appease.

In twilight, down on muddy knees,
we fill the grave with earth and sweat;
and fear we came here to appease
the grass transfigures to regret.

Ten Minutes of a Day

redbreasted nuthatch on suet

Japanese knotweed, old brittle stalks
slowly falling down

midday bright sun
morning accumulation of snow
settles under its own weight

Billie Holiday on radio
heavy, sad, distinctive voice
so far away from here

beyond vernal equinox
dark-eyed junco chases another

snowmelt drips from roof

To My Readers

i listen to you breathe while you're reading
the earth is round   it's spinning
ok
but i go to amusement parks
i know round and spinning
i have a woman who is round and spinning
she tells me i'm her only one
she tells me i'm her very first
her son the immaculate conception
c'mon
i write poetry   i know immaculate conception
i have this poem an immaculate conception
it tells me i'm its god
it tells me you're a figment of my imagination
all right
but i have a mirror above my sink
i know figment of imagination

Poor Death

in a beggar's suit sitting on your door stoop
poor death nothing but bones
it's a bony soup night after night century after century
nothing but skinny bones under his belt
death walks the alleys bumming a smoke and swig of port behind
       the dumpster
poor death if only he had a real job real meat for his soup
death standing in line at the unemployment office filling out
       application after application
HELP WANTED/full-time position available in our sewing
       department.
death sews his eyes shut
THE BEST JOB EVER/driving around in your own car making
       deliveries.
death swerves off the side of the road
WORD PERFECT CLERK/advanced WP skills/busy phones/general
       clerical duties.
death answers the phones no one calls
death types 473 words per minute no one writes back
death wears a sexy blouse and stands around the water cooler
       bent over fixing his heels
poor death in the job market night after night against rush
       hour traffic
to get home to bony soup
ah john donne poor bony soup

Gravity

as a student of physics
no one could hold a candle to me
i was like siphon pressure pumping the well of my penis
i could fire-off the laws of inertia faster than the speed
        of sound
without moving my lips
pie are square i'd argue incorrect grammar
i was the genius of the bunsen burner with a pack of smokes
and my eyebrows
tongue of my slide rule probing time and space into the cavity
of trudy kovalesky's 9 scale decimal equivalents
everything is relative i'd convince the class
except my uncle louie

this of course was light years from where i'm now sitting
minus sea level
ballasting rocks in my sofa for the next revolution of the earth

Doctor

how can i explain
i took your example
shade   quiet
i fed it shade and quiet
then closed the door
i didn't touch it
                    space
room enough to pace and dream
for a long time i knew exactly
where it was
i didn't even touch it
and these chest pains
of course i ignore them
healthy it should kick
but doctor
how does it go out
into the world without me
without me even knowing
where it is
too old and embarrassed
my juvenile delinquent heart

Chauncey's Roses

We sat by her window looking into the garden,
The stone wall gray and cold in winter light.
Sherry warmed us, made us feel nostalgic.
I wish you could have seen, she said, the sight
Of Chauncey's roses spilling over the wall,
'Most every color you can bring to mind.
They bloomed all summer, well into November;
The autumn weather was unusually kind.
One morning we awoke to find it winter,
All those beautiful roses under snow,
Like jewels—red, pink, yellow, apricot.
They died, at length, from cold, but left their glow.
She said she wished I'd seen, then made it so;
We sipped our sherry, bathed in the afterglow.

Blackberries

I picked wild blackberries as a child.
Black thimbles thick as my thumb
ripened on canes of barbed wire,
their backward-growing thorns
catching flesh, hair, clothing.
"Go *with* them, deeper into the bush,"
my father said, "don't pull away.
You must go deeper in to get free."
I learned to hold a branch away
with one hand while I picked with the other,
how to gently loosen the hold of thorns,
move with them, until they let go of me,
the tears and scratches worth the dark
sweetness of blackberries in the hand,
sun warmed, and wet with dew.

I picked wild blackberries for
my father, just before he died,
placed them in his hand.
"What are they?" he asked.
"Blackberries, Daddy," I said.
"Eat them, they're so sweet."
"You *eat* these?" he asked, incredulous.
He rolled them in his palm,
put them in his mouth at last, smiled.
"Good," he said, nodding, this man
who'd taught me constellations
he'd learned at sea, watching sails
billow toward Africa and Spain;
this man who read me poetry,
who taught me the ways of the seasons,
whose harshest reprimand was,
"Daughter, you've disappointed me."

I picked wild blackberries for you
    the day we said good-bye.
We stood on the narrow bridge
    eating blackberries;
watched pond mist rise through
    hazy shafts of morning sun;
wondered aloud at dew-wet cobwebs
    spread like lace on the grass to dry.
The words we didn't, couldn't say
    hung between us, like those
barbed canes weighted with ripe fruit
    arching at our backs.
You left, and suddenly your eyes
    were thorns, your words thorns,
I wove a wreath of blackberry vine,
    wore it as a phylactery.
Inside, pressed against my forehead,
    a scarlet leaf, inscribed
    Joy cometh in the morning.
I felt the bite of blackberry barbs, and
the pain at my center that *is* a blackberry:
hard, green, yearning for ripeness.

I pick wild blackberries for myself
in this long season of heat and drought.
The sweat rolls down my spine.
I press into the bushes, picking, tasting.
These berries are for me, and they are sweet,
their juice purpling my fingers, lips, tongue.
My loose white dress catches on thorns,
tears as, laughing, I pull it free.
I pull the dress over my head,
thrust it into the gathered fruit,
watch the violaceous color spread.
The wet dress clings heavily,
its cool wetness a joy in the heat.
I bury the phylactery under a flat stone,
mark it with a blackberry root.

Barefoot and singing I gather wild flowers,
plait a wreath, crown myself with
chicory and Queen Anne's lace.
A sudden shower washes the stain from my dress,
leaves it the amethyst of mistflower.
"Joy comes also in the afternoon," I say,
rejoicing in the warm rain.
I will not cry again for blackberries.

The Father Box

I have a box in which I
keep my father. All the parts
of him are there in no
particular order. Everyday
sometimes more than once
I pick up the box and
shake it as though I have
a small animal I've captured
from the wild. I want to be
sure it's still alive.

There was once a box turtle
I'd saved from the middle
of a hot summer road when
I was someone else. I would
keep it in another box for
an hour or a day or two.
I would shake this box, too
afraid to touch my captive
held by the ancient mystery
in reptile eyes I was also
afraid of dying.

But I found courage in the
taunts of my companions.
I tapped the turtle's shell to
make its head appear then
retreat at once like a
caveman escaping at the
last minute from an
enraged tyrannosaurus
a broken spear dangling
from its ribs.

My father's spear is in
this box. You cannot see it
but it is there among his
gold-rimmed spectacles,
his cufflinks with the
ivory insets, his 1949
fishing license that looks as
though it has just been
handed to him at the
hardware store with a
box of Eagle Claw hooks
and a spool of monofilament
five-pound test which never
got used. My father never
broke a line or got a
spider's nest or whatever
it's called when lines
become irretrievably bound.

Instructions for an Eclipse of the Sun

Black edges of memory
secret letters in a fire
rise and cover your eyes:
a double eclipse.

Warning:
Don't use binoculars even
from the wrong side.
Permanent damage may result.

Instead, pinhole an old
postcard from your father's trunk
through the hub of the Ferris Wheel
at the 1939 World's Fair.

Hold the sun over
your shoulder then
sift through the ashes,
focus light on the white part
left when the fire went out.

Eliot's Shadow

In a photograph of my flat
taken from the street below
by a much younger man you
cannot see my face behind
the glass for it is late
in the day and the sun at this
time of year insists images
upon my windows that really
don't belong to me at all.

Of course, you might imagine
reaching up to push my shutters
back to catch the fading light.
But I in turn would see that it
was near to evening and draw
the curtains closed not wanting
to believe the night would
come before I chose,
before I'd want it to.

Straight Ahead

Across the railroad tracks
in noon shadows
and rusty draglines,
the strip mine pits
make winter ponds
and the cold sun on puddles
is pinwheels on old ice
where children once skated
and in their gusty smoke breath
toasted fingers over January fires
of dead Christmas trees
and old tires stinking black,
into pots of hot chocolate

Now the train whistles
are old frozen jazz tunes
that echo through snow
on winter bridges,
these nights
when I can't sleep
from road fever burning,
hot as sun
in my body

The children
are lifers in the coal towns
working out existences
in the same mills and factories
that killed their fathers,
where the saws whine
in rhythm hysteria
as the wood dust
muffles the punch of dreams

Across the railroad tracks
the strip mine pits
make cold ponds still,
the winter sun on puddles
is pinwheels on old ice
and the tracks still
move straight ahead
glinting away in the haze
to the horizon.................

The Time Is Right

When the things I'd
        rather not think about
                begin to outnumber those
I'd waste a little
        time on if I weren't so
                consumed by thinking
about what thoughts
        to avoid completely
the categories
        blur like droplets of
                water shifting
the patterns of dust
        on the window
                so that
nothing seems worth
        the effort except not
                thinking about anything.

The time is right . . .
        this afternoon's rain
                has thinned to a fine
mist
        the dripping
                from the eaves is slower
bird songs are vibrating
        and I finally
                feel myself settle
into that deep silent
        thought I've been having
                for as long as I've lived.

So Much Life

Back and forth, fifty
a hundred times, tilling

the soil, chopping up
spring weeds, rhythm

of no-thought
in the morning sun,

only to slash open
a nest of baby field mice–

unnoticed at first
until that slight

gray movement
in the last furrow

and then five tiny lives
crawl out one by one,

three to die in my hands,
the others placed carefully

in the weeds under a hedge,
breath astoundingly fast,

whiskers a blur.
Then back to the work,

this drive
to rip up the earth,

run it through my fingers,
say it is mine,

when so much life here
hardly knows I'm alive.

After the Party
for Carolyn

In a room full of plants
you've made strong

you make the crystal bowl
ring before shutting it away.

No voices, no cars,
a scattering of snow--

stillness after
a night of rooms filled

with talk, friends
and strangers face to face.

You ping it again,
bell of dawn swelling

and fading at once.
You are that sound

a clear ringing, round and open
as you pace the house

busy with restoring
the daily order of your life.

All Night Haiku

Hot summer night—
the dog noses a June bug
buzzing at the screen door

Not expecting
such a moon
over my crabby neighbor's roof

Night game
softball soars
through swarms of gnats

After the storm
next door a candle flame moves
window to window

Sundown—
all the shadows released
from their shapes

Waking to moonlight—
a mouse in the wall
loosens a bit of plaster

4 a.m
only two peepers
still at it

All-night train—
in the darkened car
only my light on

       Honking late at night . . .
   a flock of geese
flies away with my dream

   Crickets so loud—
the spayed dog slowly
licks her scar

Top of the stairs
   pile of white laundry
      in moonlight

Big Black Car

. . . anything with wheels
is a hearse in the making.
                    —Richard Miller

I thought, You'll never get me
anywhere near that motor's flattened
skull, the hoses' damp guts, the oil
pan with its tubes and fluids; I thought,
I'll never ride the black bargello
of the treads or be locked up
behind its locks and keys,
or stare at the empty sockets
of those headlights, the chrome
grill so glazed with light it blurs—
oily, edible, about to melt.
You'll never get me into that back seat,
the ruptured upholstery hemorrhaging
batting is not for me, nor the spooky
odometer, nor the gas-gauge letters
spilled behind the cracked,
milky glass. The horn, like Saturn,
is suspended in its ring of steering wheel;
and below it the black tongue of the gas pedal,
the bulge of the brake, the stalk
of the stick shift, and I thought, You'll never . . .
But here I am, and there in the window
the tight black street comes unzipped
and opens to the snowy underthings,
the little white stitches and thorns
of a starry sky, and there, beyond
the world's open gate, eternity
hits me like a heart attack.

Blonde Bombshell

Love is boring and passé, all the old baggage,
the bloody bric-a-brac, the bad, the gothic,
retrograde, obscurantist hum and drum of it
needs to be swept away. So, night after night,
we sit in the dark of the Roxy beside grandmothers
with their shanks tied up in the tourniquets
of rolled stockings and open ourselves, like earth
to rain, to the blue fire of the movie screen
where love surrenders suddenly to gangsters
and their cuties. There in the narrow,
mote-filled finger of light, is a blonde
so blonde, so blinding, she is a blizzard, a huge
spook, and lights up like the sun the audience
in its galoshes. She bulges like a deuce coupe.
When we see her we say good-bye to Kansas.
She is everything spare, cool, and clean,
like a gas station on a dark night or the cold
dependable light of rage coming in on schedule like a bus.

Domestic Violence

The night is dark as mother's closet with its big woolens.
In the kitchen a piece of pork hisses in a black pan,
oiled in its own fat, pink and wrinkled as a baby's ass.
Not how can it be imagined, but how not, how not
to be there, under the ceiling bulb where shadows
swell, slacken--sails in the winds of an argument--
of a man with the whole dim tribe of womanhood.
To the left, the parlor, the bulges and ruptures
of broken springs and stuffing, the davenport's
red velvet like the blush of blood that comes
through the crushed ice on the cooler's dead pike.
Along the split rail fence, the white hens bloom
in a line, pale, squat little ghosts, and the far door
of the Pentecostal church is all light and holler;
the uncontrollable pleasure of blessedness dies
to the low shiver of the hymns, then the reverend's
fist pounds the air as though to make someone
who is getting up stumble and fall down again.

Since you left
I find myself needing
to relearn what things
will disappear
and what will remain
stone seems stubbornly persistent
ice is cold and hard
and fragile at its core
the day passes
you are gone and
I remain to touch
familiar surfaces
that still ignore my touch
the rain and wind remain
as unchanged as when
I was a child and knew
their coming and going
without knowing, certainly love is
not new or the need for it
or its light or eclipse
yet everything is new in sudden
shifts of light to shadows
in the thin vibrating air
of fading memory
changing as smoke
changeless as the moment
the same and different
as a nagging question
whose answer I have
yet to learn
perhaps it is
nothing but getting
the questions right
like a child's questioning
sweet, simple, and unanswerable
and yet we try our best

we tell them
why the sun shines
the sky is blue
rain falls down
people fall in love,
out of love, suffer, die
as if the answers
make sense and will
not vanish like ghosts
in the morning

The Johnstown Flood

Near the trestle table of a flea market dealer, strewn
          with china doorknobs, an ebony parasol handle,
fantastical dented silverplate—detritus washed up
          from the wreckage of some rural estate—
I'm browsing in a book, the third (and cheapest) copy
          I've found today, a bestseller in 1889, clearly

much referred to, its spine split, pages cracking,
          from habit, to a rotogravure of an uprooted elm
skewering a farmhouse's front door. It's an account
          of an old calamity, "A History of the Johnstown Flood,"
that I'm drawn to, in October, 2001. By then, events
          aren't canceled, but the crowds are sparse.

From every other dealer's table, radios stutter news
          of work crews digging through pulverized concrete.
Not much business, says the dealer, glad for my shadow
          eclipsing his display. Our silence is companionable,
becalmed by the smell of old paper, by the dumb endurance
          of so many small, well-worn personal effects.

The frightful aggravations which followed
          the coming of this torrent have waked
the deepest sympathies of this nation and of the world,
          and the history is demanded
in permanent form, for those of the present day
          and for the generations to come . . .

The accepted figure is 2,209 dead. Some bodies were found
          dangling from treetops, though most were pounded
deep in mud by the blast of water. All remembered the stench
          when workers torched the drowned horses and cattle
to spare the living from typhus. Smoke dulled Johnstown for days,
          just as in Lower Manhattan. Every unimaginable disaster

has been dimmed by another. Some future will see our losses
        surpassed. Will condemn our rhetoric as unequal to the occasion
as a Victorian journalist's. I want their kindness. So I will not slight
        the grief of those unsmiling people, dressed for posterity
in their bowlers and bonnets, posed on top of Johnstown's ruins,
        each gripping a tightly wrapped black umbrella.

Song for My Father

I. Duende

Had they been written, the words my father spoke
would not have filled a page, the loss of blood
addling, as though he'd suffered a stroke:

desire betrayed by unformed sound.
When my father slept, I tried to read,
though mainly I stood by his window,

the tenth floor of Mount Sinai overlooking
Central Park in full bloom. One afternoon,
a helicopter dragged a giant flag

above apartments and St. John the Divine,
above the wet and sunlit maple groves.
The pane of glass began to hum.

The flag had blessed Manhattan—
from the dismantled southern end on
up—to mark the final day of excavation.

When my father woke, his eyes focused on
a book in my hands. I tried to appear
hopeful. *Lorca*, I said. *A new biography*,

and he found a way to whisper, *Green* . . .
I heard each word: *how I   want you   green.*

II. Fermata

Northway Road divides this morning
so unnaturally I almost stop driving

to stand on parallel yellow lines. Even
September trees separate:

evergreens out-muscling the oaks
freckled in their seasonal decay.

My father has been dying
for weeks now, his memory split between

a pellucid past, a vague present—
and suddenly I'm far too conscious of

metaphor, and try to lose myself
in milky farmlands and forests,

tufts of clouds and evaporating mist,
all that remains of house-rattling

thunder that woke my daughter
from the sleep reserved for children.

In the center of my vision,
I am steadied by a God-like moon

fully exposed in a swath of daylight,
unable to burn off the unyielding fog

nor burn itself from this symphonic sky.

III. Louisiana, Denmark

Conceptualizing
        Giacometti's vision
                beyond the nature of his art,
I'm trapped in weighted shoes
        while memory recasts
                a Danish sculpture garden,
one extended, sunlit afternoon. . . .
        How easy, this return,
                even as I'm failing
to age almost fifty years—
        my father's eighty-eighth
                and last birthday—to know not

what he needs
        but what he desires.
                Manhattan in January,
too cold even to glance
        into any pair of eyes
                as we exit the Strand
where I've purchased
        a museum catalog:
                Louisiana, Denmark,
a place name as unreal as
        the legs of Walking Man,
                stepping across continents.
It's a gift, I suspect,
        more for me. We're all
                in Giacometti's City Square,
thin gray strangers
        momentarily caught
                ambling across steel ground
as if walking could define
        some magnificent effort
                for each limited stride.

IV. Brief Elegy

As though our rhododendron could reclaim its bloom
from this spring that has never been spring, the rain
so unrelenting today I'm astonished by the sun,

or that the heart could recirculate the blood
no longer pulsing in your hands
beneath your still-warm face,

your towering canvas in the adjacent room
unveils a vibrant sky, a human pulse,
and the pulse of where you've gone.

In His Garden
for Grampa

Thick as a jungle
just a tiny thing
I played
among the thin rows
"He'll never find me."

His small hands
studied tomato leaves
and bushy cabbage heads,
the same small hands
that labored with coal
and raised nine children.

Standing, staring
beneath the sun's brilliance
quiet and solemn
the scent of peppers
thick on their vines
surrounded
in old memories
I reached between
two corn stalks
to his thin legs
startling him
from Calabria, Italy.

Fiction

I make believe
that selecting the right apple
is a lesson I can teach my children
about choosing whom to love.

Take up what's golden-ripe,
glossy, pink-cheeked, I tell them,
and so firm
you're sure of sassy kickback

when teeth drive deep
towards the center.
This will keep you satisfied,
coming again and again.

I pretend that preference is not
seeded so early in the dark core
of ourselves to know it, and that it's
not destined, like a cowlick, to bend as it will.

As if we can choose what to want, invent our hungers,
or cultivate them from a foreign seed just sown,
that might cause us to hurl ourselves from safety,
and fall heavy, as if from a high branch.

Common Prayer

I can't imagine, I say to others
who agree or understand
it's impossible to know a feeling:
to discover a young daughter
cold-still in bed at morning,
having gone to sleep as usual
the evening before,
sipping the same dose of medicine
that this night conspires
with an undetected flaw
to produce death,
a strange distorting shock
to the fresh face we recall
beneath a mask
we can't remove.

I can't imagine how parents cope,
I say to others
who agree or understand
why it is I deny any connectedness
to the tragedy by even wildest thought,
so that I speak to put on notice
all of fate to look elsewhere for
understudy to this role I can't imagine,
or fathom, or figure how I might rise to
its requirements each morning, lifting up
the enormous weight of self from a bed.
I can't imagine, I repeat a common prayer
believing it may be true
that the gods might spare us
what we say we cannot do.

The Glass Eye
After "J. L.'s Eye" by Diana Perciballi

I

Sometimes it took you by surprise;
no matter what you said or how
you looked you were caught
in a lie, its unwavering
stare, out of nowhere, a conscience
precariously unbalanced
between the brown
iris and the pupil's
black abyss.

II

One night it took her
to what she thought she missed:
her own bed with him
looking down at her, or so
it appeared, her being
blindsided by the only eye
she could see in the bedroom's dark
tenderly taking her in, all of her
in to the moonlight, that speck
of white reflected
in the only eye.

III

Almost always
we took it to mean
nothing in this concentric
view could be ruled out, not even
the violence of rending
piece by piece the flesh it

desired, pierced
with an intimation of love.

Nothing was beneath it.
Nothing above.

IV

It was a god's eye, after all;
under color, its crystalline
vision again and again
turned on itself, invisible
to all of us the way we are
to ourselves, the way
we say a word
and it disappears
into definitions never dreamed.

V

In a dream nonetheless
forgotten, the multitudes
follow him—
their shoulders, their bobbing heads
eclipse the other eye, hips
spooning hips underneath,
the beast moaning.

The Falcon Club
for Jareth

I imagine your small fist
striking the pillow, the fluffed-up
effigy flattened by one blow
after another.

Give it to me.
Let me have it.

Was it Italy
where the ceiling fan whirled
the dark into a blur, an arc
of insomnia spinning
even into the light? *Too late*
to go back, I reasoned then, the premise
of unresolved arguments in the kitchen
long lost to cigarette smoke, my fist
pounding their points into the table,
my drunken rages unable
to sustain themselves above your mother's
answers, the clatter of porcelain
and silver at the sink.

I imagine your eyes
open, my diatribes oblivious
to your dreams of flying, the both of us
in the pandemonium
denying what exists, waiting
for the Falcon's next
edition to save us.

Love is just
another criminal enterprise. Uncertain,
the Falcon rises now above the metropolis,
his anger at the monstrous
shadows below a source
of his intent, his furious descent
into himself, fists flying.

Now comes the victim
and the vanquished hardly distinguishable, the victor
as incomprehensible to himself
as he was to begin with. A heart
as if illustrated in these pages
beats out of itself
a pair of wings.

Your small fingers once
gripped my forearm like talons.

Look.
Here you are in midair, an infant
in a floppy white hat floating above
my fingers. This photo
captures your laugh,
the trust that you would fly.
Laughing too, I appear
crazed with certainty.

The Hug
for Beckett

As though I were about to leave
but never would go, never really go,
I feel your arms almost in disbelief
wrapped around me, your strong hands
pulling the cumbersome weight
of my torso against yours, my heart
the palpable clock of being
your father turned back
twenty-five years.

Intangible fears survive
in your embrace; your hands
grip the shirt on my back
as mine grab yours, the little shake, the almost
indiscernible aftershock
of what brought us here: marriage
and divorce, the brute force
of the mind mending
the heart's losses.

I remember only now
the quiet latching of the door lock, the cold
air that November day catching my breath
                              dispersing it
in clouds no sooner visible than not,
the bare trees
branching out, the gray sky
endless.

In the stillness
of so many days since,
your five-year-old eyes question
promises swirling in the blood, the confluence
of your mother's and mine, the undivined
force of the flow.

What is there to know
of my going? Undefined still
are the drunken and maniacal
rantings after midnight in rented rooms, their walls
the stage of shadows, suicidal
in the morning light.

What right
did I have to leave, you might have asked—
the years of your small palm in my grasp
an anguish I will never see the last of.
What right now to return?
The question burns, your diminutive
footprints in the snow melted long ago
dissolved like mine
and impossible to track.

What right
do I have other than love
to assert—which cannot think
clearly of itself and which, instinctively,
comes as I do now
to feel yours.

Hold tight, my son.

Sharp Angles of Light

On the ferry two men speak of pink flamingos
that perch in Sitka spruce and draw tourists
to argue whether photos of plastic are real.

* * *

Between Eden's delight and the nonsense
of Utopia, we enter life's bargains
unknowing and are wolves, mosquitoes,
bears. Mountains clap hands, ravens
bless our chimneys, seals bark greetings—
why can't we see perfection till it ends?

* * *

A heart must turn corners and trust
the fierce geometry of angles whose blood
rushes dark as mountain streams
on the steep north face. It must submit
to the care of rivers and peaks
and allow geography to bend, tear, reform.
It costs a life to belong in this place
where December is dim, the light
acutest at its vanishing. Compressed
distance. Bronze snow heaped
on high horizons. The avalanche comes
when snow hangs heavier than the angle
of the mountain. June days so long
they forbid the aurora. Warmth
when rays escape the angle of the mountain—
the mountain closest in morning, the mountain
that exalts a man but makes his house small.

* * *

Three times the size of Texas,
Alaska—with fewer living species
and fewer miles of paved roads
than Rhode Island.

* * *

Moose need swamp and willow,
bears need square miles,
auroras command the dark.

* * *

In his saloon Jefferson Smith put twenties
inside two wrappers of his many bars of soap—
he asked his sidekicks to find the planted bills
and boast, allowing him to sell each other bar
to stampeders drinking at the bar for a dollar.
This was Skagway 1898, a great big dollar!
Soapy Smith's parlor is one of the false fronts
meeting cruise ships of prospectors who want
to imagine the gold rush where men made laws
against prostitution while they demanded it.

* * *

Back East, people choose whether
to live on a high floor or below,
to eat Turkish or Thai,
to shop at dollar stores or boutiques,
to go acrosstown or downtown
by taxi or bus,
to see a play or a film,
which bridge to cross.

Here the sunrise chooses
and the wind.
The mountains choose,
and the eagles.
The whales choose
and the salmon
and the stream.
The rainy mist chooses,
and distance decides,
and time is irrelevant,
and—if you want to—
you accept the idea of order
in Skagway. If you want to
you give up doubt,
turn corners, bend angles,
see what's real.

Call Me Ramona

I am wise with clear eyes or I'm the old man
        at lunch in the park who takes off everything
but his bikini and socks. I close my eyes

and arrange the living room, moving the sofa
        a quarter turn. My dream loses a son
from the grocery store aisle to the circus

where elephants want someone to remember.
        Some thoughts have glue on them.
My mother packed my head full of underwear

labeled *virgin cotton.* I need a sound-track
        with red music that dances. Give me
a new, exotic name.

Boots

I want to wear combat boots,
the big black ugly thick-soled
cumbersome kind.
Only I'll fly in them.
I'll let my hair grow long
and bleach it a brash blond
and perm it into
a frizzy, untamed mane.
I'll dance down
the halls of school
in my boots
and my long flowered skirts
with my wild hair
flapping in the breeze,
and I'll say "Out of my way!"
to the first person I meet
and "Have a nice day"
to the next.
I'll jump up on the desk
and do the two-step
in my boots
and sing
if I please
with my hair swaying in time.
I'll do whatever I want
and wear whatever I want
and say whatever I want.
I'll be me
in my combat boots
and crazy hair.

Auction

I hold her hairpin in my hand
whose house this is
pink lingerie still in its box
her house I trudge through
mink coat on the bedroom door
photos on table tops of
who are they?
who this woman?
her house, her couch
her clothes, her hose
her jewels and tools
and pans and plants
all doors open
closets, cupboards, drawers
basement to belfry
no nook or cranny
safe from curious eyes
I hold her hairpin
picture wiry white wisps
fastened loosely
all her life
loose like that now
sprawling
for all to see
for all to buy
cheap for the bidding.

One Day, What You Said to Yourself

Winter. Two trees in the yard of Friends Seminary
are without leaves, stark in their denudement.

The world glazed with cold, the homeless argue
in the park, their angry voices leaving them more naked.

The trees, the limbs of which held foliage, branch
and twig that winter freed, ride higher and higher,

angling into the sky and sun. But you had tired of
the bare data, the nictating perception which crowed

like a bird, *I live*, exuding the old lyric order of the world,
so that a corner was turned, the image bedded in stealth,

to emerge neither for nor against. Only some principle
you wanted without war or hope for life better than

a privileged fold in history such as the powerful make, rather
something just there in the interstices, call it a moment,

the fragment, the sweet taste of her in the second
person, for the record, later the ambush. You

encountered the trees and the trees met you and won.

Stanzas Without Ozymandias

Who finds the pedestal finds the poem.
To know time had its ruins, its knowledge.
The traveller was fortunate.

And now sand has its texts, its mica
and feldspar, its fulgurites and beaded quartz.
The heart a display case, the eye a catchment.

Granules adhere to fire-drawn surfaces,
mineralled and glassine—acolytes of the grain
fused to a speech of unwarrantable sermons.

Wind and lightning storms roll the high dunes
into long trenches, into tides of erasures, now
smoothed to a nothingness—an abyss for the geometer

who mourned the mirror's lack, who hungered for stars
hidden in the dark behind the day's brightness.
Hard to remember what tribes wandered with Moses

or even who invoked that sere alchemy when Jesus disappeared
for the numbered days of an older Flood, or what tempted
the saints to sit in their aloneness at the ledge? Unawares,

the bush burned and the mirage shimmered. Solitude of those
who entered, who sought earthly want, though they wandered
in the skull of an angel, in the trepanned and bleached spaces,

remembering only the colorless semblances of their desires.
So now to place a word on it, like a bit of mica
winking in the sun. And now to place time on it,

as though time were the handwriting of the object's moment.
Effacement in the grammar impelling one to be only a shadow.

Vocational Training

There were many such compacts:
the oscillons and quarks
formed atoms that formed particles,
sand grains and jaguars,
and hats, many hats,
and tennis shoes
and sprawling cities.

And there were hearts
that corroded
on the syllable's tin,
and siren-curators of loss,
not overly bemused by order,
hawked their translations of dross.

And we wanted to talk,
we wanted to talk,
but the sounds
were surrendering themselves
to the object's private cunning.

And so we sang,
and we sang,
as banished rhapsodes
used to sing,
about the painted vase
and the molded head,
about that one possession,
our dispossession.

Spring Poem Roethke Saginaw 2002

You of the grave's greenhouse, lost son
writ in the roots & tendrils of Michigan,
you of selvers, stem-smuts, Prussian roses—

when I ascended Papa's steps into your boyhood home
they were smothered in pollen,

& last night, first visitor in your high brass bed,
I dreamed that those acres within crazed panes
still existed, somewhere, I could breathe them

within such Time as for a few moments seemed
a delirium of blossom.

Horns

When their army unpacked to remain here,
their goods were stacked halfway up our mountain.
Our sure-footed sheep peered at crates and artillery with interest,

but kept their distance, making new paths to avoid the soldiers.
The sheep nor we knew how long these occupiers would be here
with their atrocities & chocolate bars,

but the rams' horns did not curl into this question,
the ewes' rhythms did not falter, and lambs were born,
though there were losses to drunks at target practice.

During the day, we farmed, at night we sharpened our knives
and welcomed smugglers with news from other villages.
They told us the foreigners, though well supplied for now,

were stretched thin, and wolves were at their heels.
They told us to wait another winter. They asked, with a wink,
if any sheep had consorted with the enemy.

Words

Wind in the fur of living buffalo dead
ten thousand years ago. Imagining one,
trying to imagine him: It's spring,
this bull's fur patched, he's shedding,
his longest hairs ruffle, he's grazing,
head down, but watchful for wolves. . . .
Yes, gusts lift patches of fur on his neck,
flies lift from grasses, sunflowers
brush his flank crusted with mud,
sun clots in the thickest tufts of fur.
Winter is elsewhere in memory, this
is what is, grass for its mouth,
invisible odors of flowers, air riffling fur
with the promise of sustenance over
the long, slow, instinctual migration.
& now night falls. & now Time
cannot preserve the beast's fur, or ours,
& now words are fur shed
in prairie spring ten thousand years before.

The Modernization of Jennifer

I thought I could count on the absolute in my name—
the two n's snuggled together like jovial hills.
In this was my error—nothing is absolute.
In a decade the letters liberated themselves
and split, left for more eloquent, ethnic shores.

I'm tired of sharing with a rally of females
and their issues of lust—their corrugated dialogue
in every romance novel I've ever read.

Guinevere lived a nobler life
until she fell in love with the wrong man—
restless, her crises cracked around her.
Who wants to wear a halo? Nothing is absolute.

Younger girls with urgent hearts wear it
singular, sleek. It's not fair. Age runs rampant
and I've reached an ugly edge, paled with comparison—
my apple doubly poisoned.

Surface Tension

We have slept too long in silence, nothing left to see
but the yawn of light on carpet, through draperies—a
sort of bundled quiet in the bedding and cats, tiny
hours, motes of dust in the air. Nothing down on paper

this time, your days away like waiting for a boat
to come to shore, the lapping water rolling in
and splashing my feet. Wake, soon, teach me your
passioned bristles, body of models. Oh let's dream

longer in the closed air of this morning universe and
fragile desire. Let's rip open the one wonder
of our bodies, unshaven and freckled, let's forget how
spring seems late and the laundry isn't done, why it

is never finished, that somehow in our minds there was
always this sloughing, feral leaving of what wasn't us.

Manual Alphabet

The Starbucks on the corner near St. Mark's is packed
so we sip in milliliters, scrounge change
for refills that barter more time. My body's unhinged
from a trek across concrete in flip flops, the big sack

of books and lipstick I lug everywhere. Coffee
revives even in the purgatory of July.
I take notes on the New Yorkers outside—
a mohawk the color of oxidized copper,

eight pregnant women, a man seated
with his newspaper, a grocery bag
bobbing from a tree branch crag
like a thought balloon. We greet

the photographer, the deaf man selling pens,
his manual alphabet we call to our hands again.

Lot 43

Here, in the litter
Washed up by death, values are re-assessed
At a nod from the highest bidder.
                    —C. Day Lewis

used to be home, a viable address before Death
drew the damp out of the cracks, however hermetically sealed
Now the home has gone out of the house along with the
            Oriental rugs
rolled for storage and before the auctioneer tags all else for sale

Like good Romans we've packed our household gods,
the Lares and Penates of my father and my mother;
taken out what is real and ancient and wise,
leaving to the laughter of strangers what is costume
and rhinestone and Depression glass; the yellowing lace,
the empty jelly jars for just-in-case, the dolls I never loved
and no prince will ever wake, the gracious garden gone to seed
It is winter anyway and never again will we rake acres of leaves

We leave in our wake memories of happy days
and magnificent magnolias drunk with dew
and the still warm ghost of my mother
rustling through her closet of purple clothes
and the colder ghost of my father
hanging up his miscellany of now rusty tools

We twist the key in the lock, lean back to secure
Death behind the door; not looking back, we face the drive,
knowing life goes on elsewhere in lesser addresses,
carrying with us moving pictures we can play in our heads

My Red-Winged Blackbird

Must everything whole be nibbled?
                    —Annie Dillard

He's dying
close to spring
on last year's leaves

Across a mourning coat
of black, bruised-now wing
birthmarked from the nest
is spread October's scarlet-
gold never guessed so real
as this with pain

I'm told he does not know
nor will accept from me
a home to die with dignity

Yet tonight I keep my lamps
alive and warm
for in that woods
not far from me and dawn
this bird
howls alone and unaware
that at his end is rest

False Spring

On the first day the mercury hit 50,
tidal waves of young poured from the high school,
spraying laughter bright and high on the street.
Into their eddies—carefully—a woman waded,
head bent against the crash of spring voices,
gnarled hands clutching her drugstore catch.
Oblivious to robins and jagged crocus spikes,
she wore wool—brave, defiant scarlet—
a warning beacon in the Jordan almond colors of the young.
Mauve, pink, lime and yellow,
their spindrift energy crackling the air,
they parted for her prow,
needing more years to read her red semaphore.
"You can never be too warm," it said.
"Wait. It's only March."

Lightstream Passage

You begin as rivers are begun,
> and as aware of truth as of water,
> you do not attempt else;
>> And you learn

> the secrets of oxbow,
and hands wetly discovering
>> my body
> which is now soil, waiting
my words, which are now grasses, submitting

>> You become a familiar in your lightstream
>>> passage,
> and I, as runnel,
> become sooner, losing soil and
>> grasses to you,
>> a life.

Transitory

The evanescence of music
Subscribes to the pleasure motive:
What's good is the momentary chord,
The towhee's double eighth notes,
Here and gone like the taste of Jamaica mangoes,
The scent of sweetfern on Forkston Mountain
One primary blue and yellow day in July.
Even pleasure remembered
Lasts for memory's moment only.

The skin can't hold strokes.
We hedonists must make love
Again and again.
The bliss of grapes and almonds
Needs refreshment, else we would starve.
The species sanctions our philosophy.

This doctrine serves for pruners, too.
Her off-key folk songs,
The guitar chords changing a bit too late,
Vanish gratefully into the air.
The memory of his infidelity
Has softened and blurred,
Time having erased its outlines.

Things that last longer—
Marble Athenas, the myth of the Fall,
Orion's constellation, hydrogen atoms—
Seem to support a solider thesis,
But they, too, vanish without echo
In their own scale.

Our Ancestral Gatherer Sends Endorphins

The cluster of blueberries is plump in my palm;
The feeling of fullness comes not from eating,
But from picking and fondling berries till my fingers are blue,
The way the feedmill clerk sifts corn through his funneled fist
While standing on one foot by the barrel,
His eyes unfocused on the distance, half-smiling,
And only half-hearing the customer;
The way kids scoop up unshelled nuts from the basket
Just for the pummeling of wooden balls on their skin;
The way a woman stops her sewing to dip into the button box,
Finding odd pleasure in the repetition of round edges
Rolling over her knuckles.
People play with a pocketful of change,
Fiddle with paperclips,
And so lay a hand on some ancient gate.

Cutting Edge

On some days like this one
The edges are so sharp
They cut scrimshaw designs
In your bones.
You don't want to forget—
And you won't—the glimpse
Of yellow dappled with black
That colors the lesser fritillary
Between its scalloped lines
As it opens and closes its wings
A little too fast for you to grasp
The pattern.
The colors of the whole earth
Are more surprising than the colors
Of Sistine Chapel Sibyls after the
Demi-millenium cleaning.
Even leftover rice in a plain white
Bowl cold from the refrigerator
Is a marvel of delight.

Twice this week a perfumed wind
Sweet with clover or tasseled corn
Called me wide awake
Too early with too little sleep
After cruel dreams.

On some days like this one
You want to forget—and you do—
The clutter of blood and string
Between the sharp blue air
And your own white bones.

To My Own

The lapping cadence of an Irish poet,
his measured footfalls and air gently stirred
by the pace brought me face to face with Morpheus,
until from the rolling sea of stanzas, one lost
word lain fallow these five months
rose up with such force I gripped
the sides of my chair, rocked
by a sound that might have come from you.

Hayfield. You walked down to it. You called
the herd of horses up from it. You skied
across its rises and dips, counted its clover leaves,
rode bareback through its tangled grass.

Still, this sepia scene does not define you; nor
do you speak in the sharp straw snapping
underfoot. Your words shine with the strength
and frailty of silk, music . . .

The clarinet case is closed. Your sixteenth notes
gave up their grip on the night air, and fell
to the forest floor. A deer will come
upon them and prick its ears.

The horses are sold.
The last of your father's memories
mix with ground fog, soon to burn off
in a harsh morning sun.

Incalculable loss.

No words will remain for this.
But oh, my daughter, the hayfield,
the empty, barren hayfield,
is still here.

Prerequisite
for Charles Schultz

Good grief: an oxymoron come to life
From pages drawn and quartered, inked and dyed,
Where readers sought themselves and, laughing, sighed
As their frustrations, phobias, and strife
Played out in miniature before their eyes.
Can grief be other than completely bad?
Can that which sears the heart from all it had
Be partly good? There is no compromise.
There is, however, one redeeming grace,
A balm to place upon the sorest spot,
One truth pain cannot weave into its knot.
When mourning comes, it stands upon this base:
Endearment is our bedrock, our relief;
Only those who love are granted grief.

Forecast

Tonight you throw gravel at my bedroom
window from a distance of 30 miles. I can
see you as clearly as I can hear the pebbles
pounding the thin pane, an impatient sound
from someone so good at waiting.

You gaze up from below, cigarette flipped
to the side, arm crooked and hard, squinting
into the moonlight, gauging distance and force.
Two stories above, I try to assess your purpose:
Is this a call to elope, or a more modest
request, an assertion of rights, a reminder
patience is a cheerless virtue?

Outside, old slush puddles under grey ground
clouds. Remnants of broken icicles criss-cross
the walk. I place my palms against the glass,
melting frost, clinging to your image even
as I feel the manifest drilling of sleet.

Empirical Atlantic Countdown

Grizzled seagulls glance sideways
gliding over the beached and pickled horseshoe crabs.
Heavy with the rank smell of renewal,
a vulture takes its eyes off the honeycomb,
ninth-life litter of a dead cat,
to dig its beak into a backpack
of maggots, latex condoms, and Heinz ketchup.
The borough's disposal company employs
a mechanized membrane to rake
over the irretrievable swill of commerce.
Crabs get buried under hotdog wrappers.
Crosses on chains get crushed with sand dollars
and castles in an unenviable stench
that claims everything back to a new genesis.
By and by an updraft of perfume sweeter
than the rumored breath of a snow leopard
permeates what always remains, the remains of remains.
I fall on my knees, black grains of sand
sifting through my fingers, and apologize, dear Plato,
but what I see around me refuses to defy
description. What I don't see, does.

Korespawndance
for a fire-cherry

How to organize a world—pianoforte, vibes, keyboard, pencil—
    make an arrangement with the emancipated blossoms of
    Spring.
Springing up after a fire, food for birds and Others. Bobwhite
    eats it. Moose. Chipmunks. Partisans. Grouse.
    Amused and aroused, a bear approaches the fruit with a
    fire-hydrant—this needs put out before the clearing is
    doused with dementia. The fire-hydrant is orange. A
    dalmatian offers his categorical imperative of piss.
    Smokey's neck is turning blue.
Blowing in the wind, birch and aspen tune their leaves to
    birdsong. Sun and rain copulate in white petals. Hansel
    wants Gretel in the moss. He sticks his head into the
    oven while she dies as deep as she can, and eats out her
    own womb to give him room. In and out of the house
    with no doors, wind is the breath of a stranger, keys for
    show, the hurricane sucks its own eye, the shore is the
    water.
Doors and love are parallel, she says, two banks inseparably apart
    equal a third. I say the Ojibwa have a ceremony sealed
    by candles where ghosts are sent for dreaming, where a
    translucent crow carries from the Temple of Apollo the
    silver tongue of Cicero stolen from the deathmask of his
    mirror.
Or, how many of you are there—12, 14, 16, 18—I want to tap
    them all with the tip of my tongue, and burn a map of
    the years across your pelvis with an invisible foreskin
    of invisible ink.
To think that you can leap into my lap like a little lamb and lick
    my neck. To think that when you puff your pipe, your
    lungs become a nest of ants' white eggs. To think
    that when you hear the golden horn of the Angelus, that
    I am your aphid and your child, and that love at four-ten
    is perpendicular.
The lairs of existential bears, or even Pooh-bears, exist beyond
    the control towers on the other side of the honeysuckle,

behind the Prunus pennsy......., undetectable as sleep in
the cavernous vortex of the underworld.
Earth gave Omolu as a remedy for smallpox and AIDS, gave the
inner, bitter bark of bird-cherry, gave you to me as a
girl-Christ with a splinter in her tongue from licking her
own cross.
At the berm, we have eaten pemmican, we have eaten umbilical
cords, we have eaten the sacred, willowy dark of aspirin,
we have eaten sweet fern and wintergreen, and captured
the black locust in our throats, we have eaten each
other's tails thinking we were eating our own, we have
fended off the La Goons of Kalifornia, and meshed in
the thick Trickster-mist where the penis does the crawl
as if in the river Styx, have analyzed Virgil's berth-place
snug under the stone-yellow T-shirt of a wolf fairy-
tailored as a grandmother, and even once discovered
love horizontal in seaweed in a basin of amber.
Conjure the answer far away from the signature. Conjure
jasmine at night, burdock and night-flowering nicotine,
the privileged cucumber as remarkable. See the horse's
neck, its blood trying to pulsate out into the universe.
The all-else is artificial, conceptual, a black condom
virtually in white noise, hovering between a black boot
and a red sock. Parallel. Unplugged. A negative.
Look. Down for the answer. Your throat churning with words,
the tub throbbing with liquids, the continuity of
everything into the knot-2, a luxuriant, lackadaisical
chain of being, circular, you may be the first
constellation in the world to give birth to a sailor
from a conflation of source and mouth.
Lips labiate bless you labyrinth, let's say an egg exploded from
the prodigal tastebuds of your flesh, from the felt of your
brain, from compromise and promise. Let's make it
practical, not lyrical. No storks, but forceps.
The family is Rose. Christen you a rose, Bird-cherry,
the sun will rise to this occasion again and again,
the hydra dedicate her spontaneous tongues.
Letters decompose into letters. Eyes into blossoms.
Love decomposes into life in the third person.

The Swimming Pool

All around the apt. swimming pool
the boys stare at the girls
and the girls look everywhere but the opposite
or down or up. It is
as it was a thousand years ago: the fat
boy has it hardest, he
takes the sneers,
prefers the winter so he can wear
his heavy pants and sweater.
Today, he's here with the others.
Better they are cruel to him in his presence
than out. Of the five here now (three boys,
two girls) one is fat, three cruel,
and one, a girl, wavers to the side,
all the world tearing at her.
As yet she has no breasts
(her friend does) and were it not
for the forlorn fat boy who she joins
in taunting, she could not bear her terror,
which is the terror
of being him. Does it make her happy
that she has no need, right now, of ingratiation,
of acting fool to salve
her loneliness? She doesn't seem
so happy. She is like
the lower-middle class, that fatal group
handed crumbs so they can drop a few
down lower, to the poor, so they won't kill
the rich. All around
the apt. swimming pool
there is what's everywhere: forsakenness
and fear, a disdain for those beneath us
rather than a rage
against the ones above: the exploiters,
the oblivious and unabashedly cruel.

Wife Hits Moose

Sometime around dusk moose lifts
his heavy, primordial jaw, dripping, from pondwater
and, without psychic struggle,
decides the day, for him, is done: time
to go somewhere else. Meanwhile, wife
drives one of those roads that cut straight north,
a highway dividing the forests

not yet fat enough for the paper companies.
This time of year full dark falls
about eight o'clock—pineforest and blacktop
blend. Moose reaches road, fails
to look both ways, steps
deliberately, ponderously . . . Wife
hits moose, hard,

at slight angle (brakes slammed, car
spinning) and moose rolls over hood, antlers—
as if diamond-tipped—scratch windshield, car
damaged: rib-of-moose imprint
on fender, hoof shatters headlight.
Annoyed moose lands on feet and walks away.
Wife is shaken, unhurt, amazed.

—Does moose believe in a Supreme Intelligence?
Speaker does not know.
—Does wife believe in a Supreme Intelligence?
Speaker assumes as much: spiritual intimacies
being between the spirit and the human.
—Does speaker believe in a Supreme Intelligence?
Yes. Thank You.

Coleman Hawkins

That sound coming slowly as an echo
out of heartwood,
jukebox surging into body
into soul,
mortality of flesh made duly manifest.
All the local players
in the late-night spots
staying busted
when you cut into the bone—

Mr. Hawkins is,
as always, Mr. Hawkins—listening close,
absorbing competition,
through the shovel crank
and locomotive faceting of coal,
with Stomp Evans,
Buster Bailey,
even Mamie Smith's Jazz Hounds.

Back in spiky
Harlem, early dusk out on the street,
on the move
up to Amsterdam or Broadway . . . .
Weary-boned at 60, and still lugging
that old horn,
shrunk down inside
your tailored brown silk suit.

Inside, the clotted cities
folding one by one
into *Abilene, Glasgow, Witness*—
waiting in
thick sunlight not so skinny
but alone
with your apricot brandy
and your sack of Chinese food—
pure logic arcing
east onto the train out of St. Joseph.

Blue in Green
for Bill Evans

The skeleton is yellow
where the dead seal's caught in tidewrack

across the great expanse of tidal blue,
half-buried like the pieces

of a shattered contrabass.
Blue chalked onto tablets

propped up there with charcoal sticks,
near the dog someone's

buried in the circle of pale shell,
basso profundo

for two gulls who peck dead starfish
in the backwash

running in in runnels up the coast.
An ocean comes in bands

of green then surreptitious blue,
tilting through loose blues

blue then black on the horizon,
here on the great lost coast of California.

Clouds trailing rocks
into the mouth of Shelter Cove,

stretched out across a roaring grand piano.
No one can remember

who composed this song
one woman on the beach

will sing her own song into,
the man stretching out

along the beach house
floor still putting chords together in his head,

a kind of anagram,
blue-tempered mental rosary,

sent sailing through blue coda
to Osaka. Such repetition comforting

for all its homely charm,
reminding him the world goes on & on.

Old Women's Shoes

Unbeatable fortresses.
Sturdy.
Enclosed.
They covered the feet of the women who
lived for the giving.

All tied up and
toned down.

Useful to hold in.
To hold on.

I dreamed one night of a field
dusted over with twilight.
Planted with rows and rows of old women's shoes.
Turned upside down.
Staked to the ground.
Glistening with frost.
Impaled
among the tomatoes.

Duende

Too quickly I lifted the
sheets from my mother's bed.
Weightless
they rose to be gathered and washed.
But I could not remove
from her bedside table the
Bottle of liquid, syrupy red
lacking the power to ease her pain.
Spoon
Swab
Water glass, almost full, straw leaning.
Rosary beads finally resting.
For weeks
Telephone ringing.

So I Stood By and Watched

So I stood by and watched
and you were unwinding
that endless bandage
and those bloody stains
bloody brown rusty
grew bigger bigger
and flashed more often

you were weeping
so helplessly
so silently
so lonely
What could I do?
I stood and gazed
at that descending
growing cloud of gauze

It ended suddenly
        the end
                slipped off

        there was no wound
your skin was clear

~

He returned from the backyard
           and went back to bed,
his feet still cold from the nocturnal grass.

lighter than the room,
      than the grey bitter pillow cases,
were only seams
    of the street outside
  between the running curtains

and pity
  which one shouldn't feel
pity
was reaching for the dark head
    that still smelled of tobacco
        in the pit in the pillow

The Coal Bin
for Robert McGuire (1871-1960)

Every year before the start of school
and the new heating season,
in preparation for Mr. Gontarski's delivery,
my chore was to prepare the coal bin
by shoveling what little was left
from the back to the front—
a busy-ness I'm certain my mother planned
for those last hot August days.

I wore a handkerchief like a bandit
in a Saturday western—
a ten year old's idea of play.
Alone in my 8 x 6 chamber, its walls blackened
with decades of dust, I was a coal miner.
The small window under the front porch,
held open by a single hook, was the only light,
the only source of fresh air, and served
as an exit for the dust I didn't breathe.
Tongue black, hair black, black circles
under my eyes, hanky wet with black spit—
hard symbols of my playful pride.

Twenty-five years after leaving his tools
at the foot, my grandfather's veins
turned to anthracite, the roof of his mind
collapsed like pirated pillars under the city,
his coughing blackened the pillow,
I became a black face with no name,
and I finally realized what I loved in him.

At the Hay in Curneen

What happened I am neither able to explain nor forget . . .
we were working at the hay
       late one evening in Curneen
       far back in Mayo
an odd sight, I,
stranger with a hay fork and a willingness,
unused to such late summer light,
circling the field in measured steps
       primitive precision
       relative silence
       diminishing circles
       reducing the field
I paused, not to rest,
something had drawn my attention
south toward Lough Conn and Nephin.
Turning, I saw a fist of light grasping the edge of the evening,
squeezing the landscape
until the green ran no longer green
but sadness blue and all the blue
sadness running off until the horizon
blended and I was a reflection
in a beautiful blue sadness
and I was one and separated and different from everyone
and I saw all shades of blue never seen before . . .

Then Martin John drew me back,
and the ghostly shapes of haycocks
and the cut fields to the south
looking like brown patches on a quilt,
and I
were not the same.

Late Light Edge of Women
for Stephanie

Driving through Bolinas. You with the heart ache. Someone
you loved here. We headed south and still came here among
these houses formed in wood and glass. He had a famous uncle
architect, you said. All the houses are eccentric. Sky-Shore-
Mountain fall together in shards. You might have lived here
and every jean torn couple-flowerpots-neighbors waving-wind-
washed fence . . . but I see only beauty without pain. As a blue
day transforms . . . sunset, breeze, purple morning glory, another
window on the Pacific. I take in your memories without
comment. All these old loves we must face alone. Words
smack dead against that rock . . . Soon it is evening on the
beach. We step out. Letting ourselves dissolve too. Dogs
leap after sticks. I pick up small stones and shells. Wet sand.
Seaweed. Salt. The tide almost to our shoes . . . Nothing is
permanent is the adage that terrifies . . . Things fail so much . . .
Yet still there is this. Two friends on the beach. You begin to
forget the past and stand, thumbs in jean pockets, face the sky
opalescent now and the waves darker, fiercer. Tomorrow you fly
back to Zurich and finance. I go back to the desk. Time
breathes through us . . . pulls together and then apart . . . I try to
remember your green jacket, the air . . . leaving small moments
of joy without conclusion.

Sonoma

It was a time when hearts were dead
          to symbols of love
symbols of love did not exist
          what offerings they were
Along the California coast
          in winter fog and dark
otters still dive for urchin and abalone
          they float on their backs
cracking the shells they place on their bellies
          with rocks they hold in their hands
as otter wisdom would have it
          The kelp torn by storms
washes up the beach . . . sloshing rootless
          meaningful at the moment to protazoa
a wheelbarrow full of them

Penance for Acts as Yet Uncommitted

The science/religion room always
Smelled like the holy water
We were sure sister Marcillia
Used as perfume.
Her thick cataract glasses amplified her eyes
Making us believe it was her she meant
When she'd say "the eye of God misses nothing."
When she caught big John taking lunch money
And made him stay after
His balled fist didn't look so menacing
As it rubbed fat tears.
At lunch she hit me upside the head hard enough
To knock milk from the red cardboard container and my nose.
Trying to be tough "what'd I do"
Then quickly apologetic "Sister."
"In case I missed anything McHale."
As Liz walked toward the ice cream line
It happened the sun hit just right
Making her yellow shirt transparent.
I had to look, study, notice she wears a bra.
In that moment I believed I knew.

Peeling

There are pear skins on the floor
you peel them raw and naked
loops and miles stream about the legs of your chair.
Trod upon, they are snakes
and benign dragons beneath
the feet of a saint.

The knife you use is small
its handle dulled by
hands and hands and
handing down.

Its blade is the size of your little finger.

The flayed buttocks of the pears
slump browning in a bowl
while a fellow is stripped.

To pair up.
To pair down.

Sweet meat clings to the skin trails,
despising separation;
the peel must be carved away as
darkening geometry scars the curve of the flesh.

The paring knife
fractions the solids into slices almost
transparent at the edges.

Juice weeps over your fingers.
Your hands too will brown with age.

The Night I Killed Robert Bly

The night I killed Robert Bly,
the trees burned blue.

I asked him for fire
and the question killed him.

He disjointed himself like an orange,
strings of pithy sinew connecting his traveling parts.

His hands left first, breaking and squealing away from his wrists
only to disappear on the backs of crows.

The feet dug in, snapped the legs off at the trunk
and began an hysterical troika of leaves and sugared pug noses.

His head rolled off into the wet grass
like a stampede of silent bison.

A stone lay where his throat had been,
his burnished unspoken answer.

I kept the rock and used it as a red checker
in an ongoing game with my Grandfather's ghost.

One day, an intact Bly squeezed himself out of the kitchen
        faucet
and silently asked for his voice back.

New plums converse in the language of bees.
We three eavesdrop
and tend an old garden rife with cockscomb and the icy tails
        of comets.

Nail Bag

When a cleared farm wore out or washed
in three to seven years, the soil
bleached and threadbare, they just burned the barn
down for the nails and moved on,
wagon banging buckets, babies
howling, oxen straining at fords
and ridges. To the next claim. And
once the trees on that acreage were
girdled and felled, they burned the logs
and plowed the ashes around stumps,
bringing in enormous yields from
the singed ground. Then took out the sack
of nails like slivers of crystal
that hammered right would summon
wilderness into new structure.
As though all husbandry and home
were carried in that charred handful
of iron stitches, blacksmithed chromosomes
that link distant generations.

Moving the Bees

When the owner of a place died,
the keeper of a row of hives
on hillside or orchard middle,
before the body was carried
out, before even a wreath hung
on the door or any other
sign of mourning, the bees had to
be moved. In January cold
or March wind or summer dark the gums
must be shifted an inch, a finger
width, from the place the keeper left
them, or the colonies would die
or swarm and leave, as though all ten
thousand humming workers in combs
and crystal lattices, compacting
honey from the trees and fields in
morning music, must register
the fine displacement of a death,
shift in sensitive alignment
with the sun and seasons, down to
the least egg and cell and sparkling
atom of sweetness, to start
the new dispensation in an
altered relationship to house
and woods and prevailing air,
and show the changing order now
the old one had passed away--
and the universe was moved.

Elmer's Seat

Elmer sits for years on the bank
above the meadow, watching his
cow graze. There is a seat pressed in
the leaves that seems the bed of some
animal scooped out of the hill
and shaded by the margin oaks
and white pine grove. The nest is both
leaf-lined and needle-cushioned, new
with every wind. He grazes
his cow in the spring-glade and watches
her hour by hour and afternoon
by afternoon, not moving, still as
when he lay two days in Flanders
mud and bodies, playing his corpse
and watching the sky change sides. Ground
squirrels work around and rabbits
and woodpeckers gather and leave
while hepaticas shine and leaf
out into summer as he looks
and the Jersey changes spots and
trees color and airplanes get higher
above and quieter until
they are almost invisible
except for cobwebs floating down.

Feather

Tripping the light fantastic
when the air is so soft.
      Do bugs turn over on their leaves
for snoozing, as I do,
a book open at my heart,
in a lawn-chair
          on this new platform?
"Sturdy," says Larry.
      "It's not going anywhere."
Too sturdy for any foreseeable necessity,
which is my way.

Just a mystery,
      in which a man . . .
two women . . .
a dog as sentinel observer. . . .
      Maybe the witty detective
can solve it, then go home.
      The book's now fallen to the platform
at the chair's side.
Maybe I'll wake up again, in rain.
All joy is temporary.

Fantasy baseball?
One might think of a man
      gone sour because youth was
a disappointed trip to the rained out game,
Marilyn's refusal,
      one of a few stinging nettles
still remembered.
He just can't get shed of that one.

The memory longs to forget, blah, blah,
        in this perfect day,
nothing to say.
He went south into Virginia,
                or was it North Carolina?
Was it indeed Marilyn?
        He can't find the itch. Lust, too,
is temporary. When will it get going finally?

In the mystery,
the man takes a woman,
        the dog watches, and the other woman
hears scratching
at the door foreshadowing confrontation.
Is it a guide dog?
        Somebody winds up dead,
and in the reading
I'm glad it isn't me.

                I've been that detective,
not quite as witty,
but in the end I go home too.
        You're just a few feet away,
in the kitchen, cooking up something.

                "What happened?
At the conclusion,
was there a satisfactory solution?"
There's a feather
        on the floor at your feet,
a clue, unaccounted for.
                "Yeah,
but the dog,
it still nettles.
I can't make much out of that."

By the Glenwood
for Nina Elizabeth (1893-1993)

That old oak rocking chair
over by the woodbox
is reserved for Nina who's busy
trapping dust-filled particles
of light onto her lap.
Behind her, gray cupboards
undercoated blue, and tools:
sieves, graters, skillets,
her yellow-ware bowls, and blackbottomed
pot that once kept farmer's cheese
warm on the back of the stove.

Nina pats the piles of letters
kept on the window sill
in the Whitman's candy box,
faded letters tucked into tiny envelopes
postmarked from where nobody lives.
Outside, lilacs are gone to wood,
the phlox are overrun, and
popple saplings commandeer the fields.
She sits by the Glenwood
staring out at what she cannot see,
her hands, silk over bones,
ironing her apron
as if to smooth out time.

All of This
(sections 2 & 4)

> *All of this fleeting world:*
> *A star at dawn, a bubble in a stream;*
> *A flash of lightning in a summer cloud,*
> *A flickering lamp, a phantom, and a dream.*
> —from the *Diamond Sutra*

2.

Kwangju.
Two a.m.
The phone.

Barely a whisper says
to me he loves me

then fades,
incomprehensible

broken open
heart—

he calls me.
And we cry.

Steve said he took his hand, more like a claw than a hand,
        to pull him up.

"I just wanted to thank you," my father told him, "for being
            my friend.
        I'm going to die."

        #

Cry and cry and cry.

Maybe you already know how sorrow seeps from the sky then
runs into our arms and faces, the way it moves like an old
affliction with remorse or regret

into all that's left—

three wooden rosaries naproxen celebrex tolmetin pennies
shoes dishes in the sink the kids' photographs   my head hurts
it's his palms on my back
his all-eyes emaciated face—

Maybe you already know you must do something

so furtive
while the rain falls
lightning falls

then you're in the river
voices build and break
and nothing changes yet everything changes

then the sun is remarkable finally
and burns us so in love with it
and warms the waters
and we feel again heat in each other
as Cypriot children dance a Hora
and mercy is in short supply in Kosovo
and between us there are only these words
and a radio on a window ledge outside the Jing Jang that plays
         Hayden all night
as 747s land while the sun comes up in Madrid as hundreds
         of thousands
of faucets run and toilets flush and faces get shaved and love
         gets made
and the children sleep as the dogs pace in a slight wind that
         ripples the maples.

4.

Gone completely silver now,
watching from a distance as she always did,
Ma steps out of that wind into substance with the sun
behind her so that she is all shadow, yet I can see
she carries an apron full of mushrooms as she often
carried greens or corn or beans in those days.

"You remember, Tony," she says in the breeze,
"it was the summer we moved."

She was her worries and her molds,
her crumbling limestone.

She was rain and rheum and soaked sheets.
She was nausea and vomiting,

and hands full of hair
in her roses and wisteria,

and when she died in the stems and scree,

she resembled someone resembling grief resembling rage.

#

She comes and goes   sodden woods seep
into greens and blacks   an open window   another
floats by   she's at the curtains   her long fingers repose
with a smoke at a table   her hair in curlers   she rants
at the trees and sky   she warbles   who returns her crazy love
who are the trees   the saints in white shirts on the line
          our father
waves bread across the table   sips coffee   purses his lips
          sighs

sunrise   put spite in their eyes   and winds
out of the west   in this   another tumultuous day
in an unimaginable series   as the light has now shown the trees
to be swaying   changing their greens in this light *breeze*
a word she liked and used often   *don't worry dear*
it will be a breeze

Birth at the Orphanage of the Artisanado de Nazareth, Mexico City

A few of the boys knocked on my door
in the middle of the night:
Teacher, the pig is ready.
I followed to the cinderblock stall
where the sow lay in straw light
charged with her panting
and the yellow eyes of the goats.
Twenty boys, still in pajamas,
crowded delicately around;
one knelt behind her, rolling his sleeves.
He'd done this before.
                              Rain tapped
the crude aluminum roof
held with loose bricks;
the sow gave a grunting squeal
and the first piglet arrived, pulled out
by the boy and laid near the mother.
The other boys cheered then calmed
as his brown skin disappeared
into the pink hide; soon a row of five
lay neatly at the teats. Cinco! Rang out
over the wind that snapped the roof
like a sheet on a line. He reached in again:
the sixth was still, its limbs and snout
pale, pointing forward. Immediately
snatched up by the group, it got passed around
as they took turns trying their new toy:
a puppet pig that knew Spanglish
and could dance and sing.
It jumped, it kicked,
it sat on people's shoulders and crossed its legs,
dangling a tiny notched hoof.
The other pigs suckled at their mother,
but the puppet pig tossed its head as it spoke;
it made jokes and walked around.
They ran to the yard, in the rain and wind,
carrying the still birth like a hero,
shadows against the dormitory's glow.

A Blind Man Tours the Musée Rodin

Allowed to touch,
he fingers the open mouth
of John the Baptist,

the curls that spill the platter,
and caresses Camille Claudel's face,
her threaded cap and smooth forehead,

the eyes of stone that stare
above the unfinished block.
He traces the ribs of Ugolino

who crawls, blind with hunger,
over his limp children
strewn about like rags.

Descending Francesca's shoulder,
his hands meet Paolo's hand
resting on her thigh;

he maps her calf
and ankle's hollow, and Paolo's toes
that dig into stone.

A woman says to her child,
It is not polite to stare.
But the girl turns again

from the burgher of Calais
whose hands wrap his face in despair
and watches the man

before the Gates of Hell
as he feels the slender, muscled arms,
the arched torsos,

the lean tangled legs of souls
sprawled on the dark,
impassable doors.

Rain Writing

Rain slithers down my window in brooding
streams blue skylines
flow past in undulating hues.
I slide the window open wide, lean
into humid sky and inhale my wet city. Drenched
in the redolence of summer showers.

Seoul breathes a diluvial stew:
moist cabbage leaves, lilac trees and sewers
gurgling sweet, garlic, boiling
rice, ginseng root and rubber
shoes, concrete steaming fresh
like beanpaste and exhaust
dissolved in barley tea.

Umbrellas roost along sliding streets
with thin blue plastic on bamboo wings.
Breezes release these flapping cranes
into clouds grey as mountains.
Heaven and Earth whirl in balance
for days as long as the Han River.

Three stories below, roads rush
slick with sleepless tires and slapping feet.
Time clatters down drainpipes and drips
from tiled roofs, each drop warm
on my eyelids and the palms of my open hands.

Falling Stone

I was born in this city and she gave birth to me
the labor was long—almost twenty-two years.
I grew in her center where fourteen million converge
then shoulder their way home.
Seoul is a bowl of mountains
circles enclose on circles
windows become eyes of countless buddhas
searching for space, escape, drowning the peninsula
we slide into the Han flowing with prosperity and traffic
swirling like schools of toxic fish.

In the lurch of my airport taxi
I round a corner steeped in pungent squirming larvae
sauteed with a wide spoon—a silkworm snack
seeps through folded censored newsprint.
In winter hot coals warm gnarled sweet potatoes
and raw hands taste tenderly
a woman rests against department store glass
she is as cracked and brown as the chestnuts
she sells steaming between her frozen legs.

As a child, I sat in Ajuma's lap and together
we laughed at the flaccid fall of her breasts.
Her sesame hands caressed my hair and
plucked one strand, one stitch of hope for her family.
Eun sooni, the youngest daughter, played with me
in a gravel yard. With sewer gurgling, she taught me
Korean characters drawn in soot blackened earth.
We tossed tiny stones in summer air, a game of kongies.
Before the stone falls, I try to catch my memories
scattered across three decades ones then twos then threes then
tuck them in my carryon the stone is falling fast.

Kimpo terminal swarms with farewells
I cut through their collective grief
as the blonde child who walked through
a flock of student boys fleeing concrete classrooms
like uniformed magpies fluttering apart in V shaped ribbons.
The boarding tunnel races under my feet
a fleet of planes spews gaseous purple plumed
trails to follow in the amniotic haze.
When I'm pushed through these fuel slick
contracting lanes will I know where I am?
Will I drive north south turn left and down an alley
or will I float to the moon, spin out of orbit?
The stone is falling fast, engines scream,
airtight voices slice like scalpels
wide mouthed doors slap shut and we rip open the sky
As the air grows thinner colder
I ask my city below
can I be born again?

Bass Notes

1.

Dear Herr Brecht,
I have been looking for God.
It was not my idea.
My mother sent me
                    on the quest.
At least, that seemed her pleasure.
(Who can say
what satisfactions
a lovebearer's after?
I have been searching for years.
There is nothing to report.

2.

Because I know only fear
and fear of fear and
what fear can do
I do not think
I will know
more just
this so
little.

3.

I think I know
why (I don't of course
you jumped off that bridge
                        in Frisco
if you did.
You grew tired, Kees
of trying to orchestrate
all this late-modern nada
                    into stuff.

Maybe though you stole
back through the Donner Pass
or have you pitched a tent
in Hiroshima?

Are you flesh yet
or only bones?

Someday, mon frére
I will climb
the Great Wall
and call
your name.

Blood Rites

It's November 4 and some people are still
wearing shorts. Out of the sun, they regret it.
These skyhigh blue skies are almost blinding:
Would I have time in an atomic blast
to turn and take a final look at you?
Unmoored, we drink schnapps off Hoboken,
seaboard where doughboys embarked for one last war.
Sinatra swam underwater here
to shape notes that would sing the unsayable.
Weeks-old smoke rides New York's downtown air.
Blackened ideographs, brazenly erect,
score the desolation: flesh and blood
sacrificed to appease what belittled god?
But enough never die. The woken nod.

Pentimento

I reach to tear the faded yellow sheet
From walls that won't indulge today's desire
For crisp and clean. They struggle to retain
Their fleshly comfort, years of smells and stain.

The yellow sheet yields pink and blue bouquets
Reluctantly, revealing children's years.
I reach to tear the flaking, flowered sheet
Determined to avoid one memory.

But that Thanksgiving hangs among the shreds.
A faceless child still wavers in the paste
Her life uncelebrated, death unmourned
Until this cleaning, stripping game of mine.

Remorse lies thick before these surreal blooms.
No consolation from the sweat and stain.
I tremble, stop, think what these walls have held.
I reach to tear until I reach the bone.

In the San Diego Airport
for Dylan Annis & Samuel Cyrus David Ray

What is the rush to release a deluge of babies? In timeless eternity, souls
bear no hardship in waiting to come onto earth. By having the flow of
births moderate, everybody will eventually come here, and the here will
not be a paved-over, nature-scarred, solitude-scarce, God-denying place.
                                          —John Muir

No shortage of babies today–I count a dozen
close by and note that a high percentage
of passengers are either pregnant or pushing
strollers–or both–and several toddlers
are running around carpeted areas, a few
chased by older siblings. A boy about two,
nose pressed to glass, looks out at an airliner
as his father remarks that the plane will soon
take them aloft. "All the way up to heaven?"
the boy asks, and the father says, "No,
we come back down when we get to Denver."
But the boy frowns. He much prefers heaven.

As for those of us who have lost children,
who too often spot our own toddlers among
ghostly avatars and angelic clones who frolic
in airports or tag along beside fortunate parents
wherever we go, we know that this is a hazard
of travel–and one we can never prepare for.
Sorrow like a booby trap awaits us in malls.
Blindness might help, for one stray glance
and we're bombed back to the gates of hell.

We should love even clones of our lost ones,
but no god has taught us how. What matter
who gets the babies this year or loses them
tomorrow? Can we not counsel our envious
devil within to let them all live and even offer
a smile, and vow anew never ever to kidnap
one who might replace a Samuel or Dylan?
I stand back as the airliner lofts yet another
ancient toddler high into the heavens unharmed.

The Moment
for Joshua L. Roberts

Walking the three tiers in first light, out
here so my two-year-old son won't wake the house,
I watch him pull and strip ragweed, chicory, yarrow,
so many other weeds and wildflowers
I don't know the names for, him saying *Big*, and *Mine*,
and *Joshua*—words, words, words. Then
it is the moment, that split-second
when he takes my hand, gives it a tug,
and I feel his entire body-weight, his whole
heart-weight, pulling me toward
the gleaming flowers and weeds he loves.
That moment which is eternal and is gone in a second,
when he yanks me out of myself like some sleeper
from his dead-dream sleep into the blues and whites
and yellows I must bend down to see clearly, into
the faultless flesh of his soft hands, his new brown eyes,
the miracle of him, and of the earth itself,
where he lives among the glitterings, and takes me.

The List of Most Difficult Words

I was still standing although
Gabriella Wells and Barbara Ryan were too,
their bodies dark against the wall of light
that dull-pewter December afternoon,
shadows with words that flowed
so easily from their mouths,
fluorescent and *grievous*,
pied and *effervescent*,
words I'd spelled out to the rhythm
of my father's hoarse whispers
during our nightly practice sessions
beneath the dim bulb,
superfluous, excelsior,
desultory and *exaggeration*
mixed with his Schaefer breath
and Lucky Strike smoke

as I went down
The List of Most Difficult Words
with a man whose wife had left,
one son grown into madness,
the other into death,
my father's hundred-and-five-pound skeleton
of skin glowing in that beer-flooded kitchen
when he'd lift the harmonica

to blow a few long, sad riffs
of country into a song
while he waited for me to hit
the single *i* of *spiraling*,
the silent *i* of *receipt*,
the two of us working words hard
those nights on Olmstead Street,
sure they would someday save me.

Ontogeny Recapitulates Phylogeny

"How would you like it
if I were dancing with a dead shark?"
My five-year-old daughter asks
from the back seat.

> And I remember an old lover
> who after late night studies,
> dissections, wrapping small sand sharks
> in Saran wrap to store in his dorm room
> fridge, stopped in the middle
> of *everything* to ask if I could check him
> for pharyngeal gill slits.

She reads from her book,
Creatures from the Deep,
shouts, "Their teeth grow back!"
And bites the two-year-old
sleeping soundly beside her.

> Requiem shark fetuses
> are intra-uteral cannibals
> consuming their less developed siblings.
> Pregnant for the first time, I was enormous.
> Twins were suspected, never found.

Passing the shopping center, the 7-Eleven,
we keep moving.
My gill slits long since sealed,
I still never sleep,
moving only to keep from drowning.

Offerings

Once mistaken for a man I began to dress like one.
Tall, broad-shouldered, hair cropped close,
I could wear seer suckers, double-breasted pinstripes,

disguised, free to go anywhere I pleased.
But I rarely spoke, and was the only woman
my rich old neighbor would choose to eat with.

After a day's shopping for Mission Oak in Soho,
Brooklyn's Atlantic Avenue, we would lunch
at Alfredo's, Tom watching the young waiters

dodge toward us, in and out of tables,
balancing plates of tortellini,
cold asparagus, double chocolate cake.

He'd take a few bites, then push the plate
to me, say, "Here, enjoy."
In the gym beneath the overpass,

Saturdays, Tom and I sat ringside
as trucks ground above the barrio boys
dazed by smoke and lights,

listing against the ropes.
The bell would bring on Tom's Parkinson's--
foot scuttling, tapping cement floor,

the tremor quickly spreading to his leg,
hand clasped hard against his thigh.
I'd remember the first day he asked me in--

a small stone figure of a sleepy Etruscan
sat on a table near Tom's bed,
its smooth back burnished by his constant stroking

as if this ancient citizen
might imbue Tom's body with rest.
In the last round, the tremor passed

to a cloud of smoke above the crowd.
And I knew I'd have to make my own way home
as Tom rattled the bills he'd fold

into a fighter's satin pocket,
taking him like all the others
to spar in his living room. The street's neon--

LINDEN LIQUORS, KNIGHTS OF COLUMBUS--
banding the walls, torsos flashing pink
then green as Tom lowered his gloves,

asking to be hit.
I did his laundry, cooked, arranged poppies
in a Roseville vase,

dusted his books, and the Etruscan,
a Tiffany shade's blue wisteria
while Tom sat and watched me work.

He gave me some beads,
cool green and mottled, Mayan.
"Everything's gray," he'd say. "Make it clean."

Templo de Mars Tulum

Stone temple by the sea where
eastern shade and brisk breeze
cool sun-red arms of sweaty travelers
who make diverse observations
about this ancient university at Tulum.

Where is the knowledge Mayan scholars
discovered and catalogued here?
Where are the astronomical tables and
mathematical formulae that determined
precise alignment of virgin shrines?

Ten years ago Viking soft-landed
on Martian plains to capture
a red sunset on the red planet.
American spacecraft relic reflects
solar photons off metal landing pod.

Twelve hundred years ago Mayan priests
observed and charted the orbit of Mars
through careful measurements by the sea.

What was the Mayan word for
what we call "The Caribbean?"
      Trillions of zillions of water molecules
      mixed with salt & minerals & kelp & plankton
      — "the soup of life" —
      full of sharks & seaweed & barracuda & shellfish.

Above the blue water, we climb
onto a steep narrow outcrop,
welcomed by the cool dark shadow
angling off the eastern stone wall of
The Temple of Mars —
a planet that one day, like the moon,

will accept the footprint of homo sapien —
It won't be Christa's footprint,
It won't be mine; rather it will be an eager student
now studying astronautics at M.I.T.
or some such university,
a repository of knowledge,
like Tulum   like Tulum.

How Love Lasts

Over Oregon   an accident.
What he was doing when the door opened
wasn't reported   but whatever happened
when the copilot was sucked from the plane
he caught the stair cables and held on   never mind
the winds at two hundred and ninety mph
changing his face into a star   his eyes singing
and another sound in his head like hammered light
he held on.

The pilot when he understood what happened
(could anyone have understood what happened)
considered his options.   There were no options
not to fly lower   not to fly slower   unable to pull the man
still impossibly pressed against the outside   inside.

The pilot turned back to Portland.

Now remember   this is a true story
both know what must come next
the tilt   the descent.
What will the landing mean to a body
that's forgotten it's a body?
How will the pilot find words to tell
what he cannot believe?   Come back   says Portland
all the runways have been cleared.
The guide lights we send out   won't save you
from what you cannot even imagine.

When the ground crew got to him
they cut away the icy rags that were his clothes
they cut the cables from his hands that wouldn't open.
He was alive.

I'm the copilot   the pilot   and Portland.

Garland

Slow work at first.
She sits with a vine's mind
weaving for its own sake such
flowers as she can find   ferns
leaves   whatever comes to hand.

Her fingers find the tendril's
motive   move with it to entwine
grasses   twigs   and husks.
Stones can be jewels
or weapons later.

Nutshells   feathers   roots   berries
enough moss is a pillow.   Nests
and hives hide valuables. The skeletons
of two small birds
are lockets at her breast.

It fills her lap and falls
around her feet.   A net
a chain   does it matter it repeats itself?
Why is she crying?
She can wear it   or leave it.

Calafawnya

Involved in peripheral necessities
In which lakes certainly had a part
And why not? the man was witnessed
Buying furniture. Purportedly.
He was seen that is in a furniture store
Assumed to be same because of "pieces"
Placed about with hopeful artistry. Well,
Not *artistry* but arranged as are the bits
And pieces of the well-made story.
Obvious as a glass of water yet really swell.

There he was buying furniture
Or looking at the "pieces" placed about
By someone who clearly knew nothing
And probably still does not
Of the "craft" of display.
Believe me it was cheap stuff and very dear.
He had on a tie and seemed to belong
But he did not belong. They all knew that.
Yet he paced judiciously. And did not smoke!
He was all obedience indeed. Then
Of a sudden it began to rain of course.

Weeks later after the usual instances of living
That is, this that and the other thing
We discover him about to eat his breakfast.
He is in the middle of the saddest living room
On a metal lawn chair? It is quite impossible.
To tell. What happened? Wait. There's the sun.
And right on time. It of course began to rain.

Boy Raised by Wolves

At first I was distressed
to dip my snout in gore,
but soon I put aside my
shame and tore in two
the bloody beating heart.
We killed by starlight.
The woods were ours.

Then one day the soft-
clawed creatures came
and calmed my blood.

Now I can't name
the several scents
that blow among the birches,
or where we jerked the last kill
crashing to the ground.

Tonight I press my face
to the fence in the blue night,
waiting for you, my brothers,
where the wind is just the wind,
and the moon is a strange stone.

Fishermen at Mori Point

The sea is a man named Maynard,
a three-hundred-pound dancer, gliding,
swirling, full of grace and danger
and the sweet smell of dinner gone wrong.
Skimmers fly by, thousands, black hands
clapping silently, inches off the water.
Pelicans wheel and hack at the waves.
Gulls weep--you don't love me, you never did.
From nowhere the fishermen appear,
working their lines, whipping the swells.
Big rollers barrel into them, but
they stand, hip-deep, not minding it.
They dream of salmon tender as sunset.
And soon they're hauling them in, fat and greasy,
dragging the fresh kill up the sand,
bellies flashing whiter than midnight birches.

Now they head back to their campers and
cold beer, dragging the dead behind them
on a leash. The pelicans are gone.
The skimmers have swept past Pedro Point.
The gulls drift down the landfill,
whining for the garbage to forgive them.
The best is over, but some stay,
pacing the beach, poles cocked in the sand.
They pitch their empties into the wash,
cursing the cruel bitches they've left at home,
their back-talking brats. They pace, they read
the waves, the sky, they shake their heads.
There's nothing right or fair.
In their shallow graves, inches from the surf,
the salmon sweat and blow.

I would be the hagfish, flat and eyeless,
miles below, where light is an ugly rumor,
where the hook and line mean no more
than the detonation of some distant star.

"Fish or Cut Bait"

We torment ourselves with options,
but the *or* assures us
there are only two—that's all there is.
Any situation demands we settle
on something, for better or worse.
Unbearable for some to think
we could be of three minds,
or four, or maybe none—
the ambiguity of it all,
the casting about, like water
feeling its way along a shore,
the river dividing beneath us
while we toss our baited hooks
into its current and wait.

If We Were Trees

You would be a young totara,
flare-skirted, rising from the undergrowth.

I'd doubtless be a Rata—
Metrosideros robusta—

inoffensive seed a bird would digest
perched in the crook of your branches.

Then I would pass through,
start to grow, would flower

scarlet in spring and reach for you,
our limbs entwining.

My coiling vines would seem
safe—until you realized

they crept down from above, umbrella-ed,
massing, encasing you. We would be

two serpents wrestling in the same garden.
And after two hundred years,

you would vanish completely
inside me. I'd assume the form

of an ordinary tree,
and no one would know

you were the hollow
inside my massive trunk.

Gumbo, Hoodoo, Blues and Woe

gumbo hoodoo voodoo blues
gators in the bayou hungry as sin
rollin' their eyes, sayin' jump on in
candles burnin' at the tomb of marie laveau
everyday her worshippers come and go
notes of jazz, blarin' in the street
white folks jumpin' to an african beat
mississippi river movin' slow
catfish and mysteries down below
Black folks livin' lives of woe
gumbo hoodoo voodoo blues
razors and guns whipped out fast
can shorten a life not meant to last
gators in the bayou hungry as sin
rollin' their eyes sayin' jump on in
spices and hot sauce burnin' the mouth
in the Big Easy way down South
travelers come from every which way
most leave but some do stay
'Nawlins, 'Nawlins you's a Creole bitch
a high yellow woman and a jet black gal
a head rag voodoo priestess old as lust
shakin' a bag of mojo dust

Smokescreen

I would sit next to him
And watch smoke from his cigarette.
That was easier to watch than him.
Rising up, up, from the tip of the stick
Straight and true
Till it curled, quite suddenly,
Into chaotic swirls.
Wafting and gliding in the air,
It would settle in layers,
Then barely shift and move.

He kicked the habit;
The smoke has cleared away.
With the smokescreen gone,
I must look at him.
His straight and true life
Has also dissipated into disarray;
Hanging there,
Then swept away on a chance wind.

Going Home
for Winston Harrington

I hope the plane isn't crowded
When he travels so he can stretch his legs
Across three seats, and I hope
That nice girl I met when I went home
Is working the flight, so she will let him have
As many cushions as he wants and fix him
A special meal of only the soft stuff that he
Eats now, and smile that pretty way of hers
That even his wife won't mind,

And I hope the pilot is one of those
Exceptional BWee guys who make it seem
So easy you hardly know when you take off and
Land, just a soft bump as you taxi in, who make
Small talk for the whole trip in the parlance
Harry loves, saying, instead of turbulence,
"We just have to make a little giddy in de hole,"
So all the passengers laugh, and feel comforted
And raise their behinds and crane their necks
So they can see each other.

And when they land I want the sun to be
Shining, or if it's drizzling lightly
For a rainbow to appear by the flyover, and
His grandson to be chatting incessantly all
The way home to his house in T'un Back Alley,
And the breeze to be just laden with the heady
Smell of ladies of the night, though it's only
Afternoon. And his wife and daughter to
Stand on either side of him with their hands
Under his arms, and hold him up so he can look

Over the rooftops down to the sea, so the view
Will enter his eyes and go straight to his heart
Stepping over the bad dog that lies sleeping nearby,
And the steelband just below will begin
Its practice then, a tune he's never heard before,
So he'll forget all about where he's been,
As the whitecaps seem to rise and fall with
The music, as the arranger strikes for them
To stop! And take it from the second passage
Once again, only slower, this time.

A Betting Man

When he can't be found at the government office
Where he works, Harry's at the betting pool,
Picking Jetsam in the second to win, or
Crazy Ursula to place.

He's close to retirement now, so no one complains.
His top drawer overflows with torn-up tickets,
And what little work he's been assigned goes
To the new clerk, who learns as she goes along.

He likes the one on Henry St., where they
Know him, his white hair stark in the dark parlor,
His eyes steadfastly on the screens. For lunch
He hops over to the restaurant on Charlotte,

A card game going in the back. He has a chat
With his teacher friend, an expatriate returned.
They scold each other about bad habits, then hurry
Back before the race is run, the next hand dealt.

Harry picks his horses as he does his friends,
With blinders on. He likes whom he likes, never
Bets on strangers. Never mind who's riding
Crazy Ursula. He goes with her all the way.

Two Photographs of Mike Rieder
(The Watch Repairman)

I. 1906

You lean against a varnished cabinet
With a single knob, your thin arms forming
A chevron, your hands clutching the corners
Of the cabinet top. It is the perfect height

And width for such a nervous pose. The camera
Is in the opposite corner of the room
And your unsmiling face with its dark
Moustache is turned slightly. Can you see me?

The display case is too bright, too distant,
At the wrong angle. I cannot buy your watches.
Tell me, Mr. Rieder; do you, like most of us,
See everything in terms of your trade?

The forest, your children, the stars
Are mechanisms prone to stretched-out springs
And worn gears. With your windows blanked
By sunlight on a morning after snow, you would

Be pleased to learn that January,
Though its crystal is scratched,
Though it runs ahead, though its casing
Is tarnished, still has that blinding look.

II. 1927

Twenty years later, nighttime, and I
Am looking at you from across the counter.
You fix bicycles now (tire tubes
Hang dimly), and while your earlier life

Was sunlit starkness, this newer shop
Is lamplit clutter. There are stacks
Of books, a torn clipping of a man
In a powdered wig, and a sign that begins

"Not responsible . . ." in reverse. Your hands
Are in your pockets. Your gaze
Is confrontational as if to say, "You!
Yes, you on the other side! Take note

Of twenty-one years! Read my caption
As that is all you know of me! Notice
That small clock near the left-hand border!
It stares at you with a pale face like mine."

Dictionary in the Rain

In 1979 my grandmother gave me a dictionary,
Webster's New Twentieth Century from 1953.
Hardbound and the thickness of snow tires,
I used it first as a doorstop and then
As a stand for my speakers. I tried

To get rid of it last spring, but feared
A scandal; an unchewed dictionary stuck
In the broken trap of a disabled
Garbage truck. I thought of burning it,
But it would burn forever so I dumped it

In a squeaky wheelbarrow instead and dropped
It in the woods far from the path
Where grandma is too old to go. When my dog
Came back, her tongue tattooed
With the definition of "spectrograph,"

I saw my terrible mistake. It's true:
A rain-swollen dictionary nuzzled
By a curious deer, kicked by a builder
Of tree forts will spill its rotten
Terminology and wrong answers. Just today,

I saw an illustration of a frigate stretched
Like taffy and floating on the surface
Of a polluted stream. Last evening, walking
Through the woods in short pants,
My legs were scratched by accent marks.

Eventually (It is all my fault!)
The water table will become contaminated
And those who drink from wells will insist:
A computer is "one who computes."

"Frank Tate 1935"

I was fifteen in 1935
When we climbed Bald Mountain.
I was thirty-three.
I was fifty-two
Which means I have long been dead.
My mother packed chicken sandwiches
And hard-boiled eggs.
While she cleaned up and my father smoked,
I asked him if I could chisel my name
In the granite trail.
He nodded.
The screen door snapped behind me.
My infant daughter started to cry,
But I just kept walking until I hit the summit.
I did not want to face my wife
So I killed time by carving my name and the year.
I said to my grandson, "This is how you speak
To future generations, let them know
You were here."

"1935" sits between the dates on my gravestone
Like a robin on a clothesline.
For those who still climb the mountain
And walk the granite trail
From the transmitters to the overlook,
This was the year
Radar was invented,
Persia became Iran,
Hitler enacted the Nuremberg laws—
"Frank Tate,"
A name on which to hang a life.

Mercy

The destruction that brings an eagle from heaven is
better than mercy.
                    —Robinson Jeffers

The love of an angry man
devours; the fires
in the hill of his own undoing
move him down
blind paths of the mind's hungers
and the twisted coastline

I have known men so brutal
in love they consumed
what they touched and left
a scorched desert; but the one
who gently said never
depend on a man, who
nursed my dream of my self,
who stayed facing the door,
always halfway out, and refused
to light the hearth,
who left when the flame in my eyes
grew so strong
that his soul gave itself away
revealing its dim estate,
he was the one
whose lack laid me waste

Chicago

Here's where I want to write
the poem of the world, it's

giddy, like landing in Chicago for
a rendezvous in 24 hours

all the buildings lit up
with bars at the top

where you'll climb alone and suddenly dazzle
the indivisible businessmen guzzling

double Manhattans in an off hour
before you are due to meet the Jungian juggler

the plane making a landing, bumpy,
your beautiful daughter all grown up

back at work where you left her in Middle
America happily married but not married

to a bassoonist who adores her and occasionally accepts
maternal advice, so that's settled and you're on the loose

again, your personal junket
involving an old hotel three kinds of transport

a bus-ride into unknown countryside and a prize
for a long poem you transcribed in a daze

years ago. Now here it is Chicago, open
wide, your temporary destination

lit up, no immediate
appointments, clean sheets,

new make-up, an easy laugh, jitney from the airport
and only one of your children dead yet.

Far Afield

Toward the horizon that light
picks out impeccably
but you are too short to see
you toddle on baby-fat legs.
Head-high to grass spikes
fuzzy with grain,

you are attracted farther afield
by this stiff stem, that feathery tip,
attracted so far away from me
the back of your head
is a frizzle of sunlight,
out of focus, indistinct.

I want to freeze the grasses,
those timothys, fescues, fox tail ryes.
Freeze your height below their nodding fronds.
Fix the season ever summer, the day
today, stay the kitchen garden
at this noon of wilting greens.

The shock that jolts my womb is not
the earth the daughter stands on
splitting into fissure at her feet,
the smoky roiling in my gut
not some god on horseback
rearing with spring fever.

It is the mother's black refusal
of your turn away, my little girl.
But you thrust yourself so boldly
down the long chute of birth,
how can I let you or me
be die-cut by a myth?
Instead I watch you move through air
suffused with pollen
and chaff, your vision hazy
so I seem a smudge to you,
a cloudy thumbprint like the one
moon impresses on the midday sky.

Unless Blue

Streaming into sky through string, solitary
child swoops on a rag tail and paper ailerons

what if she could fly, open the back of her heart
into wings, what sky then, what blue

she wants most to float into would float
into her, so why did teacher have to say

Pharaoh's daughter could not see blue
no word for it, no hieroglyph

river only muddy from under the muddled shade
of canopy swagged over barge

how could she have trawled her regal fingers
through green or brown to say what Nile was

the child could not say ocean unless blue
current ocean flowed through

could not say sky, paper eagle
plunging, no wind unless blue

Infatuation II

Questions
always rose like juries
between her leaving and her
return. When she went away,
his breath would stop,
would wait, held for
days sometimes,
dared not break
the spell her
spirit
cast.

Answers
out of steam,
fluent at the mirror
scraping lather from his
scarlet cheek, breathing slowed,
himself mesmerized as
the razor's cadence
revealed
her face
in his.

Questions
skipped like stones
across the soup bowl;
he worshipped through the lunch
hour, and waited till
she said good-bye
before he'd
exhale.

Answers
out of blue-green
twilight, charmed walks
over grass-covered fields,
herself spirited enough to set
the breeze to play; he breathed in long
draughts and ached to hold her,
wondered if he blew a kiss
he would lose her
to the wind.

Second Night at Alta

Tony says, "What're you hungry for?"
I say, "What do you got?"
He says, "Are ya eatin' here?"
I say, "Should I?"
He says, "Sit right dere, Maria'll setcha up."

I sit.
Eight-year-old Maria says, "Did you wanna menu?"
I say, "I think Tony knows what he's going to make."

She brings me my cola.
He brings me a green salad with marinated onions,
hot peppers, and an acerbic vinaigrette.
A few moments later, he returns with
a red, white and green basket of bread.

I say, "Hey, how'd you know I like onions?"
He says, "I hadda hunch."

I eat my salad while Tony cooks bowl
after Friday night bowl.

He brings me a dish of penne alla vodka,
tells me plainly, "Don't stuff yerself, I got a coupla
more things I want you should try, soes next time
you'll maybe know what ya want."

The penne is perfect,
on the firm side of al dente
the sauce is slurpily good.

Next, he brings a dish of perciatelli amatriciana.
Rough chopped garlic, hand hewn bacon, barely broken
whole stewed tomatoes, red pepper spicy.
The hollow noodle, like the chunk of the sauce,
must be stabbed not twirled.

And finally, a chicken and broccoli alfredo,
again with penne,
whose fatty garlicky cheesy richness I can only pick at.
I'm stuffed.

Alta tonight is: Tony, Maria, Francesca, Timmy, Paulie,
coarse, gravel throated Neil, and,
a round little boy with a head of thick black hair
who never stops walking and speaks just once to say,
"Si, pa pa, si."

And pa pa Neil says, "This? This is Dante,
he owns the place,
cancha tell,
he's walkin' around all da time,
see,
we're all workin' for him."

Harry's Poem
for Harry Irving, December 1993

Down at Jody's General Store
I think I see your reflection
in the window, baseball cap
askew, big pot belly,
                              but it's only my own,
moving through the same space
as you did just last week, when
you sat in our living room and spoke
of the old things: pontils on hand-blown glass,
charcoal drawings of great-grand-ancestors
and the way these pre-winter days have shrunk
to damp, gray pools—

Better to remember you
            in longer, warmer days giving us
            one of your natural science lessons:
barefoot and stripped to shorts, you carry
the woodcock to our front porch and pass
            it around—straight and stiff,
                              its beak
all pointy and ready to peck.
                  Died for want of love, you say.
Last night you heard him
            call for any lover he could get, then in a final
                  mating dive, auger into
                              the cab of your Chevy pickup.

Remember: you
padding around your chicken barn
looking for which-its or whatcha-may-call-its
or sifting through the latest haul
from the Houston-Brooks Auction:
                              boxes of

longjohns and lace nighties
trumpets and Jew's harps
Andy Wyeth prints and Vargas calendars
typewriters without keys
keys without locks
knobs without doors
fill-in-the-blank marriage blessings
        (pre-signed by Pope Pius XII)

48 plastic boxes of rosary beads strung with
        genuine olive pits from the Garden of Gethsemane
along with two alligator roach clips and three dozen
        pairs of rubber gloves with an invoice from 1960
            marked "Albert Einstein Hospital"

the same pattern necktie
        in forty copies and five different colors
wax stencils and pencils engraved
        "Sisters of Mercy"

and once, an organ that hardly had its wind
        but sold for a dollar and you couldn't say
No

You—
        putt-putting around
        in circles, lost

        in thought
        always the same place

        in our memory
        in our own long twilights:

        the mower on the meadow
        the light burning in the barn.

Identify

I
Kicking it
and my teeth are dry
and I just left my dinner
in the bathroom.
(Ever wonder about brussels sprouts and a turkey sandwich?)

My boyfriend licking silica,
asks why I'm nervous
and
"When are you going to start writing again?"

Where are all those pretty, fuzzy corners
to these rooms now?
Even my children are dangerous,
sharp and insistent;
droning flies.

II
This pockmarked Welshman died before I was born
He scraped my soul with vodka and singing suns.

What a team we would have been!
Dueling desks and ice cubes,
typewriters and limes.

III
Which world will love me more?
Which world will grind me finer?

Contributors

Margaret Almon lives in Lansdale, Pennsylvania, and works as a medical librarian. She was secretary of MPWA in 1996, a guest reader in 1996 and 2000, and taught a workshop on using the five senses in poetry.

Juan Amador, born in Rosario, Argentina, is an architect and an educator. He has written a collection of bilingual poems, *Mosaic/Mosaico*, and has read his poetry in Pennsylvania, New York, and California. Juan is anticipating the publication of his English version of a collection of tango poetry.

Richard Aston, a native and current resident of Wilkes-Barre, Pennsylvania, has belonged to MPWA for over 20 years and published a poem or two each year since joining. The latest of his engineering textbooks can be accessed online.

Elizabeth Balise grew up in Springfield, Massachusetts, where her identity as a writer got its start. She has lived in Scranton, Pennsylvania, for thirty years, working at numerous waitress and human service jobs while she raised her daughters. She returned to college to become a teacher.

Karen Blomain, a lifelong Pennsylvanian, teaches in the Professional Writing Program at Kutztown University. She has four books of poetry, one novel, and numerous poetry and prose publications. A translator and essayist, she has taught in France, Russia, and Austria and is a consultant for the Geraldine R. Dodge Poetry Project.

Thomas Kielty Blomain, a longtime MPWA member, is author of *Gray Area*, a collection of poems from Nightshade Press.

Victoria Torres Cays was born in Quito, Ecuador, and arrived in Pennsylvania in 1963. In 1970, *Revista Ecuador* published her first poems in Brooklyn, New York. Maggie Martin introduced her to MPWA. She is now director of Bicultural, Bilingual Arts Center in Stroudsburg, Pennsylvania.

Nancy W. Comstock lives in Mehoopany, Pennsylvania.

Michael Czarnecki lives with his wife and two boys on Wheeler Hill in the Finger Lakes region of New York. He began writing poetry in 1967 and, since 1994, has made his living as a poet and editor of Foothills Publishing.

Craig Czury, a native of Wilkes-Barre/Shamokin, is author of 15 poetry collections, including *In My Silence to Justify*, and editor of two anthologies, including *Fine Line That Screams*, from his Pennsylvania Prison Poetry Project. He works as a poet in schools, homeless shelters, prisons, hospitals, and community centers throughout the world.

Nancy K. Deisroth's first published collection was *Blackberries*, and a second, *Sympathetic Harmonies*, is near completion. Her poems have appeared in the anthologies *Coalseam* and *Got Verse*, as well as *The New York Quarterly, Potato Eyes, Endless Mountains Review*, and others. She is a freelance copy editor who lives in the Poconos.

Michael Downend is a playwright, poet, television writer, and actor. He was awarded a Rockefeller/OADR Playwriting Grant and Playwriting Fellowships from the Pennsylvania Council on the Arts. He is a member of the Writers Guild of America, the Dramatists Guild, and PEN International.

Michael Edmunds is a graduate of Marywood University. For the past 30 years, he has worked as a professional musician, currently with "Cat and the Fiddle." He resides in Dundaff, Pennsylvania, with his wife, Janice.

David Elliott is Professor of English at Keystone College in La Plume, Pennsylvania. He currently serves on MPWA's Board of Directors. His poetry has appeared in many journals, and his haiku were included in Norton's *The Haiku Anthology*. A collection of his haiku, *Wind in the Trees,* was published in 1992.

Lynn Emanuel is the author of *Hotel Fiesta, The Dig,* and *Then Suddenly –*. The latter was awarded the Eric Matthieu King Award from The Academy of American Poets. She is Professor of English at the University of Pittsburgh, and Director of the Pittsburgh Contemporary Writers Series.

Ray Emanuel is a psychiatrist working at Walter Reed Hospital and currently living in Silver Spring, Maryland, with his two children, Galen and Katie.

Sherry Fairchok was born in Scranton, Pennsylvania, in 1962. Her first book, *The Palace of Ashes,* was published by CavanKerry Press in 2002. In 1999, she won The Ledge Chapbook Award for *A Stone That Burns*. She was a featured reader and workshop instructor for MPWA in April 2004.

Sascha Feinstein won the Hayden Carruth Award for his poetry collection *Misterioso*. He is Professor of English at Lycoming College, where he chairs the English Department and edits *Brilliant Corners: A Journal of Jazz & Literature*.

Paul A. Ferraro lives and works in Forest City, Pennsylvania. A Viet Nam veteran, he has written about his experiences. He was the founder and editor of *The Endless Mountains Review*.

Paula Gannon resides in Clarks Summit, Pennsylvania.

Gerard Grealish founded MPWA in the fall of 1978. His poetry and literary criticism have been published in *The Ontario Review*, *The Bad Henry Review*, *Contemporary Literary Criticism*, and other publications. A criminal defense attorney, he resides in Dunmore, Pennsylvania.

JoAnne Growney founded the River Poets in Bloomsburg, Pennsylvania, in 1994. In addition to her own writing, she co-translates Romanian poetry, most recently, *Sora mea de dincolo / My Sister Beyond*, by Ileana Mălăncioiu. Her poems have appeared in *ByLine* and *Hanging Loose*. In April/May 2003, she was artist-in-residence in Skagway, Alaska.

Suzanne Harper of Scranton, Pennsylvania, is currently a senior instructor of English at the Worthington Scranton campus of Penn State University. She has had numerous poems published in a variety of small periodicals and has read her poetry to a number of organizations, including MPWA.

Michael Heller has written a number of books over the years, among them *Wordflow: New and Selected Poems* (Talisman House, 1997). His work has appeared in numerous periodicals. He lives in New York City.

William Heyen lives in Brockport, New York. Recent books include *Shoah Train* (Etruscan Press) and *The Rope* (MAMMOTH Books). He edited *September 11, 2001: American Writers Respond* (Etruscan Press). He has won NEA, Guggenheim, American Academy & Institute of Arts & Letters, and other prizes and fellowships.

Jennifer Hill-Kaucher's first book of poetry, *Questioning Walls Open*, was published by Foothills Press in 2001. A Pennsylvania Council on the Arts roster poet, Jennifer conducts poetry residencies and workshops throughout the state and recently in Ireland.

Barbara Hoffman, nurtured in Rochester, New York, has coached creative writers at Marywood University for 35 years, encouraging students to join MPWA. Her MPWA involvement began when founding mothers and fathers had no gray hairs or panic attacks when reading in public. Recently, she republished and updated *Cliffs of Fall*.

Jane Julius Honchell is Associate Professor and Director of Theatre at Keystone College, a former staff feature writer and columnist with *The Scranton Times/Tribune*, and she is also the author of three prize-winning plays. She is a mother of two and resides in Glenburn, Pennsylvania.

Jesse Stormont Hunter read in MPWA's first season at Scanlan's Saloon. He published two volumes of poetry, *Definitions in the Figure 3* and *Sixtree Burnings//An Exodus*. In the early 1980s, he was an ordained Methodist minister serving congregations in Susquehanna County. He died in a car accident in May 1985.

Susan R. Ide taught English and writing for more than ten years at Keystone College and was a recipient of the Margaretta B. Chamberlin Chair. The college published a collection of her poetry following her death in 1993. She lived on a mountain in Mehoopany, Pennsylvania, and she was an avid MPWA supporter.

Susan Luckstone Jaffer, originally from New York City, has worked as a newspaper editor and freelance writer. She has been a member of Mulberry Poets & Writers since 1989 and has served as secretary. Her poetry has been published in *Yankee*, *Potato Eyes*, *The Lyric*, and *Light*, among others.

Kerry Shawn Keys comes from the Susquehanna Valley, Pennsylvania. He currently works freelance as a poet, translator, and cultural liaison, and has over 40 books to his credit. His most recent book is *Conversations with Tertium Quid*. He received the Robert H. Winner Memorial Award from the Poetry Society of America in 1992.

Thomas Lux is Bourne Professor of Poetry and director of the McEver Visiting Writers Program at Georgia Tech. He also teaches in the Sarah Lawrence College MFA program. His newest book of poetry is *The Cradle Place*, published by Houghton Mifflin in 2004.

Rick Madigan is Associate Professor of English at East Stroudsburg University. His poems have appeared in *Poetry*, *Crazyhorse*, *The North American Review*, and elsewhere.

Maggie Martin is a rostered poet with the Pennsylvania Council on the Arts Artists. She has been Poet in Residence at the V.A. Center in Wilkes-Barre, Pennsylvania, for many years. A performance artist, she formed the series "Maggie Martin and Friends" at the Deer Head Inn in Delaware Water Gap, Pennsylvania.

Irina Mashinskaya, originally from Moscow, U.S.S.R., was the first-prize winner at three international Russian poetry contests in 1995, 2001, and 2003. She is the author of four poetry books and a book of translation, *Parallel Rivertime*. She lives in New Jersey and teaches Mathematics, Earth Science, and Russian in high school.

John E. McGuigan is a retired secondary school teacher and a rostered poet with the Pennsylvania Council on the Arts Artists in the Schools Program. He is the author of two collections of poetry, *A Wonderment of Seasons* and *Part of a Geography*.

Maureen McGuigan lives in Scranton, Pennsylvania, and is a poet with the Pennsylvania Council on the Arts. A member of Mulberry Poets & Writers Association since she was a little girl, she participated in many of the group's events, including the 2003 Jazz and Poetry evening and Visual Poetry at the A.F.A. Gallery.

Bernie McGurl is a fourth-generation native of Lackawanna County, Pennsylvania. He has worked in the railroad and construction industries. He is the president of the Lackawanna River Corridor Association and active in several other community organizations. He was a co-founding member of MPWA.

D. Brett McHale, a fifth generation Pennsylvanian, works in Taylor, Pennsylvania, and lives in Waverly, Pennsylvania.

Loretta A. Mestishen teaches Theatre at Penn State Hazleton
and Speech and Drama at Reading Area Community College.
She studied poetry at Bennington College, where she received an
MFA in Writing and Literature. Her poetry and prose have
appeared in *The Philadelphia City Paper, b.*, and *Schuylkill Living
Magazine*. In addition, she has written and directed plays and is
a visual artist.

Robert Morgan, a native of western North Carolina, has taught
at Cornell University since 1971. His most recent book of poetry
is *The Strange Attractor: New and Selected Poems*, and his most
recent novel is *Brave Enemies: A Novel of the American Revolution*.

Toby Olson has published eight novels and twenty books of
poetry, including *Human Nature* (New Directions, 2000). The
recipient of fellowships from the Guggenheim and Rockefeller
foundations and the NEA, Olson's novel *Seaview* received the
PEN/Faulkner award in 1983. He lives in Philadelphia,
Pennsylvania, and in North Truro, on Cape Cod.

Carolyn W. Page has two published collections, *Troy Corner
Poems* and *Barnflight*, as well as hundreds of poems published in
U.S. and Canadian litmags. She and her husband, Roy Zarucchi,
reside in Albuquerque, New Mexico, where they write mysteries,
their latest being *The Montezuma Murders*.

Anthony Petrosky is author of *Red and Yellow Boat*, *Crazy Love*,
and *Jurgis Petraskas*, for which Phillip Levine awarded the Walt
Whitman Award for the Academy of American Poets. He
divides his time between Gwangju and Pittsburgh, Pennsylvania,
where he directs teacher education at the University of
Pittsburgh.

Marilyn Bogusch Pryle studied education at the University of
Scranton and has an MFA from Emerson College. She has
taught middle school English in Philadelphia, Boston, and
Kathmandu, Nepal. Her poems have appeared in various literary

journals, including *The Florida Review*, *International Poetry Review*, and *The Spoon River Poetry Review*.

Jennifer Purvis was born and raised in Seoul, Korea, and lived there for 22 years. In 1996, she moved with her husband to Pennsylvania, joining MPWA shortly thereafter. A middle-school counselor, she now resides in Jacksonville, Florida, with her husband and two children.

Brian Quinn lives in Scranton, Pennsylvania.

Charlotte Ravaioli, MPWA member since 1988, is Vice President of Academic Affairs and Dean of Keystone College, La Plume, Pennsylvania. She has poetry published in *Endless Mountains Review* and has participated in WVIA's Poetry Minutes in 1990, 1992, and 1993.

David Ray's recent books are *One Thousand Years: Poems About the Holocaust* and *The Endless Search: A Memoir*. His awards include the William Carlos Williams Award twice, The Nuclear Age Foundation Peace Award, and The Maurice English Award. He taught for many years at the University of Missouri, Kansas City, and now lives in Tucson, Arizona.

Len Roberts is the author of eight books of poetry, the most recent being *The Silent Singer: New and Selected Poems*. Recently, BOA Editions published *Before and After the Fall: New Poems by Sandor Csoori*, Roberts' translations of the renowned Hungarian poet. He teaches English at Northampton Community College in Bethlehem, Pennsylvania.

Ann LaBar Russek received an MFA in Poetry from the University of Alaska. She is an award-winning poet and has published poetry, non-fiction, and children's fiction in many publications. She was the first place winner in the MPWA Poetry Competition in 2002. Currently, she lives in Chester County, Pennsylvania, with her family.

Jan Selving resides in Stroudsburg, Pennsylvania, and teaches in the English Department at East Stroudsburg University. Her work has appeared in a number of literary journals, including *The Denver Quarterly, Ploughshares, Crazyhorse,* and *The Antioch Review.* She is also a visual artist, and has shown her work nationally.

Rondo Semian, a West Scranton native, has served as MPWA President from 2001 to 2004. A co-founder of MPWA, he has also held numerous other offices in the group over the course of three decades. Currently a bookkeeper, he holds a BS in Physics from Stevens Institute of Technology.

Annette Basalyga Sloan has taught Latin in the NYC school system and literature at the University of Puerto Rico, Penn State, and Marywood University. Her poems have appeared in *Columbia, The Spoon River River Review, Commonweal, Atlanta Review,* and *Beloit Poetry Review,* among others, and she has won several awards.

Gilbert Sorrentino lives in Brooklyn, New York.

Brent Spencer is the author of *The Lost Son,* a novel, and *Are We Not Men?,* a collection of short fiction. His work has appeared in *The Atlantic Monthly, GQ, Midland Review, Epoch, US 1 Worksheets,* and elsewhere. He teaches creative writing at Creighton University in Omaha, Nebraska.

Michael Steffen lives in Bushkill, Pennsylvania. He has had work published in *The Ledge, Rhino, Potomac Review, Paper Street,* and *Birmingham Poetry Review.* His first full-length collection, *No Good at Sea,* was published by Legible Press in 2002. A second, as yet untitled, collection is forthcoming from Manifold Press.

Lamont B. Steptoe was born and raised in Pittsburgh, Pennsylvania. He has authored nine collections of poetry, including *Crimson River, American Morning/Mourning, Mad Minute, Dusty Road,* and *In the Kitchens of the Masters.* He read for MPWA in 1990 and 1992.

Sherry S. Strain, currently serves as the Assistant to the President and Senior Director of Institutional Effectiveness at Keystone College, La Plume, Pennsylvania. A native of Texas, she moved to Northeastern Pennsylvania in 1988 and soon became involved with MPWA open readings. She served as Vice President of the organization in 1995.

Mervyn Taylor, born in Trinidad, teaches high school in Brooklyn and teaches also at Lang College and The New School in NYC. His work has appeared in journals such as *Poetry International*, *St. Ann's Review*, *Sulfer and Rattapallax*, and *BigCityLit*. He has published two volumes of poetry, *An Island of His Own* and *The Goat*.

Scott E. Thomas is employed as Head of Information Technologies at the Albright Memorial Library. His poems have appeared in *Mankato Poetry Review*, *Orphic Lute*, *Kentucky Poetry Review*, *Plainsongs*, *Confrontation*, *Sulphur River Literary Review*, and other journals. He lives in Scranton, Pennsylvania, with his family.

Madeline Tiger's most recent collection of poetry is *Birds of Sorrow and Joy: New and Selected Poems, 1970-2000*. She has taught in the New Jersey Writers-in-the-Schools Program since 1974, and has been a "Dodge Poet" since 1986. She became associated with MPWA through Karen Blomain, whom she met at the Columbia School of the Arts in 1986.

J. C. Todd, of Philadelphia, Pennsylvania, is a contributing editor for the online poetry journal *The Drunken Boat*. Her chapbooks include *Nightshade* and *Entering Pisces*, and awards include a Pennsylvania Council on the Arts poetry fellowship and two Leeway awards. This fall she will be the poet-in-residence in Annapolis, Maryland. Her first reading as a featured poet was at MPWA.

Dennis Toomey lives in Scranton, Pennsylvania.

Dan Waber's work hasappeared in *Vispo*, *Riding the Meridian*, and *Möbius*. When not working on the abecedarium that is logolalia.com, he's on Undernet's #poetry channel hiding behind the nick [brick].

Roy Zarucchi has published two books of poetry, *Sparse Rain* Pygmy Forest Press, (1992) and *Gunner's Moon* Cider Press, (1996). He is the former owner and editor of Nightshade Press and co-founder of *Potato Eyes* literary arts journal.

Claudia Zehner lives on a farm at Porchlightponds with her partner, Debbie, her mother, Dorothy, and their dog Kijana. Zehner's current interests are being, pruning, and xeroscaping. She is working on a book concerning the care of her mother.

Credits

Margaret Almon: "The Suit of Women" first published in *Hayden's Ferry Review*. "On Renoir's *Sleeping Girl with a Cat*" first published in *Comstock Review*.

Juan Amador: "It Is Better in the Train Station" first published in MPWA's 1990 *Poetry Minutes*.

Karen Blomain: "Recorded History" won third place in the Allen Ginsberg Poetry Competition.

Thomas Kielty Blomain: "Asterisk (**Apologia ad Infinitum*)" and "An Old Woman's Ears in Temple" appear in *Gray Area,* ©2004, Nightshade Press.

Victoria Torres Cays: "Diá de Todos los Santos" first published in the *Stroud Courier Literary Supplement* in 1980 at East Stroudsburg State College, East Stroudsburg, Pennsylvania.

Craig Czury: "Gravity" was published in *The Prose Poem: An International Journal*. "Doctor" was published as a FootHills Broadside.

Michael Downend: "The Father Box" was published in *Red Pagoda Press*. "Instructions for an Eclipse of the Sun" was published in the *Endless Mountains Review*. "Eliot's Shadow" was published in *Nightshade Reader*.

Nancy K. Deisroth: "Blackberries," first published in *The New York Quarterly*, # 45, 1991; also in 1991, in her chapbook *Blackberries*.

David Elliott: "The Time Is Right" first appeared in *Passages North*. Portions of "All Night Haiku" first appeared in *Hermitage, Frogpond, Acorn, Northeast* and in *Heiwa: Peace Poetry* in Japanese and English, edited by Jiro Nakano and Brien Hallett (Honolulu: University of Hawaii Press, 1995).

Lynn Emanuel: "Big Black Car," "Blonde Bombshell," and "Domestic Violence," from *The Dig and Hotel Fiesta*, ©1984, 1992, 1995 by Lynn Emanuel. Used with permission of the poet and the University of Illinois Press.

Sascha Feinstein: "Song for My Father" first published in *American Literary Review*.

Paul A. Ferraro: "In His Garden," first published in *Cornerstone Magazine*.

Michael Heller: "One Day, What You Said to Yourself" from *Exigent Futures: New and Selected Poems*, ©2003, Salt Publishing; "Vocational Training" from *Poetry New York*.

William Heyen: "Words" will appear this fall in an anthology, *American Zen: A*

Gathering of Poems edited by Ray McNiece & Larry Smith, published by Bottom Dog Press. "Spring Poem Roethke Saginaw 2002" will soon appear online in *Poetrybay*.

Barbara Hoffman: "Lot 43" first published in MPWA's 1990 *Poetry Minutes*.

Jane Julius Honchell: "False Spring" first published in MPWA's 1990 *Poetry Minutes*.

Jesse Stormont Hunter: "Lightstream Passage" was first published in *Sixtree Burnings//An Exodus*.

Susan R. Ide: "Transitory," "Our Ancestral Gatherer Sends Endorphins," and "Cutting Edge" appeared in *Poems*, ©1997, Keystone College.

Susan Luckstone Jaffer: "Prerequisite" was published 2004 in Volume 84, Number 1 of *The Lyric*.

Thomas Lux: "Wife Hits Moose" and "The Swimming Pool" from *Half Promised Land*, Houghton Mifflin, Boston, 1986. Reprinted by permission of the poet.

Rick Madigan: "Coleman Hawkins" and "Blue in Green" first published in *Brilliant Corners*.

Maggie Martin: "Old Women's Shoes," first published in *VIA*, vol. 8, #1, Purdue University Press, 1997.

John E. McGuigan: "The Coal Bin" published in *Part of a Geography*, ©2003, Paper Kite Press.

Loretta A. Mestishen: "Peeling" and "The Night I Killed Robert Bly" were published Spring 2004 in Volume Five, Issue One of *The Mulberry Poets & Writers Journal*.

Robert Morgan: "Nail Bag" and "Elmer's Seat" from *At the Edge of the Orchard Country*; "Moving the Bees" from *Sigodlin*. Both books published by Wesleyan University Press. Reprinted by permission of the poet.

Carolyn W. Page: "By the Glenwood" has appeared in *Barn Flight*, ©1995, Negative Capability Press. First published in *Axe Factory Revue,* 1994.

Marilyn Bogusch Pryle: "Birth at the Orphanage of the Artisanado de Nazareth, Mexico City" and "A Blind Man Tours the Musée Rodin" were published Spring 2004 in Volume Five, Issue One of *The Mulberry Poets & Writers Journal*.

Charlotte Ravaioli: "Pentimento" first published in MPWA's 1990 *Poetry Minutes*.

Len Roberts: "The Moment" and "The List of Most Difficult Words" from *The Silent Singer: New and Selected Poems*, ©2001. Used with permission of the poet and the University of Illinois Press.

Jan Selving: "Offerings" was first published in the winter 1993-94 issue of *Ploughshares*. Reprinted by permission of *Ploughshares*.

Annette Basalyga Sloan: "How Love Lasts" was first published in *The Listening Eye*, and "Garland" in *North American Review*.

Brent Spencer: "Fishermen at Mori Point" is reprinted with permission from *Midland Review*, #6, Spring 1990.

Lamont B. Steptoe: "Gumbo, Hoodoo, Blues and Woe," forthcoming in *African Americans: A History Through Poetry*.

Madeline Tiger: "Mercy" and "Chicago" appear in *Birds of Sorrow and Joy: New and Selected Poems, 1970-2000*, Marsh Hawk Press, 2003; "Chicago" in *Marlboro Review*, 1997; "Mercy" in *Stone Country*, 1988, and in *My Father's Harmonica*, Nightshade Press, 1991.

J. C. Todd: "Far Afield" first published in *The Bucks County Writer*, 4:2 (Winter, 2004) and "Unless Blue" in *American Review* 30:6 (November/December 2001).

Dennis Toomey: "Infatuation II" published in *Got Verse, Valley Anthology*.

Roy Zarucchi: "Harry's Poem" was published in *Pembrook Magazine*, 1995.